Secrets of Trout & Bass Fishing Revealed

Roger Aziz

AnEx Publications

www.anexpub.com

I dedicate this book to my wife, Shirley, who has been a source of inspiration to me for over four decades.

Preface

This book is written for all those fishermen who have little spare time to pursue the finny critters that inhabit the vast expanses of water we have on this fair planet. I offer the reader up-to-date information on where to fish, when to fish, and how to fish for trout, bass, pickerel and other sport and game fish.

How to fish is the key to this book. The methods described will enable anglers to catch fish no matter where they are fishing. Fish are the same, with few slight variations in habit, no matter where in the world they are found. Over fifty years of fishing experience have taught me that the knowledge I bring to a new lake or pond is more important than fancy tackle. Knowing the fish species and applying proven techniques have enabled me to catch fish when others have failed.

To those fishermen who have to make precious the time they have astream, this book should prove invaluable.

Contents

CONTENTS

1

Taking Trout with Flies

The Fly

Not every fisherman can cast a fly line with the accuracy and grace of a Ted Williams. And not every fisherman has the opportunity to fish pristine waters where the temperature creates conditions for fly-fishing on a year-round basis.

In New England, where I've done most of my fishing, fly-fishing is usually good from the shank end of March through the end of summer on certain ponds and lakes. It is during those cool-water periods that we can most enjoy this ultimate of fishing experiences.

To catch trout on flies, you must first know what fly patterns the fish will take on a given day at a given location. Because volumes have been written on fly-fishing, I will address the subject in a manner that will enable you to catch fish, without delving into all of the deep dark secrets of this sport, which is all too often mystifying for many fishermen.

You don't really have to know about emerging insects or commit to memory all of the names of the other aquatic creatures in our lakes and ponds. A carefully selected collection of fine fishing flies are all you will need to help you to catch fish regularly.

With that in mind, let's discuss some of the flies that many fishermen have found to be reliably effective, and consider why they may be so productive. Black is a favorite color for rainbow trout. For some reason, black will bring trout out of the deepest pools to savagely attack a fly. On the other hand, these same trout will also devour brightly hued flies. And peacock herl used as body material is so buggy looking that most trout cannot resist flies tied with this exotic material.

Thanks to modern technology, we now have an abundance of man made materials that are extremely effective in enhancing old tried and true fly patterns as well as newly created patterns, some of which are entirely tied with man-made materials.

One modern piece of material I frequently use for freshwater fishing flies is Flashabou tinsel with marabou action, which is simply to say that it is very supple. The other is Crystal Flash, another sparkling material that is not as supple as Flashabou.

Both Flashabou and Crystal Flash are excellent for topping off the wings of streamer flies and in some cases it works equally well when applied to smaller wet flies. Any of the more popular streamer patterns can be greatly enhanced with these man made materials.

Gold and silver tinsels are now joined in a fly tiers materials box by holographic gold and silver tinsels that have much more flash than plain tinsel. When I began to use this material for the bodies of my Golden Demon flies it enhanced their fish attracting ability almost twofold.

Chenille, that rather bland tying medium has been greatly improved by modern materials such as Cactus and Crystal chenille and Estaz chenille. And Fishair, another man-made material has become popular as a replacement for animal hairs for the wings of many streamer flies.

Large wire head streamers developed by Joe Blazonis of Salem, NH are excellent if not unorthodox fly patterns that deserve the attention of serious trolling fishermen anywhere in the world. Blazonis is a local legend who tied so many flies in so many ways that many of them defy being named. However, it is important to note that some of the most popular streamers such as the Grey Ghost, Black Ghost, and most any other streamer can be enhanced with the addition of a wire wound head giving them weight. Furthermore, Blazonis tied exceptionally long wings on his weighted streamers, so long in fact, that they much more resemble saltwater flies in length. Despite the long wings, trout take Blazonis flies with gusto and there are few short strikes.

In most ponds that are designated "Fly Fishing Only" it is illegal to use lead-core line. The use of fast sinking line is allowed however, and this includes salmon sinking line; a level, heavy line that sinks quickly. Another way to assure that you will get down to the fish is to use two heavy weight sinking lines such as a number 12 super fast sinking line spliced with another fast sinking line.

The point to keep in mind is that a fly box need not contain all of the 20,000 fly patterns that are on the books. A dozen or two of the most proven flies in several sizes will suffice. Your fly patterns should offer you the opportunity to present both dark colors and bright colors at your pleasure.

Let us start with a list of proven fly patterns. Because local (Merrimack Valley based) fishermen invented many of these patterns, they are not discussed in the authoritative books on the subject. I am presenting these dressings here for the first time to a national and international audience. Those flies that are already in the books, unless changed to a large degree, will not be defined here.

My Favorite Flies

Black Gnat. In the smaller sizes the black gnat is probably a shoo-in as a favorite fly. Gnats are found almost everywhere in the Northeastern United States. For the best results with these imitations, they should be tied sparse.

Claire's Creeper. Originated by Claire Ignatio of Lowell, Massachusetts, this fly is excellent for both brown and rainbow trout.

Dan's Leech. A good fly for all three species of trout, this fly was originated by Dan Esty of Lawrence, Massachusetts.

Ed's Fly. A good rainbow trout fly. This is another black-bodied fly that will work in pond or stream.

House Fly.   This is a rainbow specialty. A dark fly that works well in streams and ponds containing rainbow trout.

Lamma.   This fly is super for all species of trout. It is best when tied with a red body. A green body, however, will also work at times.

Little Devil.   Favored by brown and rainbow trout, this fly is bright and attractive. Best results are obtained by fishing it slowly.

Little Woody.   This fly is one of my favorites for trout. It is tops for all three species of salmonoids found in the Northeastern United States. The Little Woody is tied in both male and female patterns, the difference simply being that the female has a red tail and throat. The male woody was originated by Jack Cooper of Salem, New Hampshire, and the female version by the late Larry Roy of Manchester, New Hampshire.

Mink Fly.   This is a nymph that will take brook and rainbow trout regularly. It is simple, and should be tied in small sizes only.

Peacock Nymph.   A good fly for all three species of trout. Fished slowly, it will account for a great many fish when they are selectively feeding.

Red Head.   Originated by the late A. I. "Pal" Alexander, this small sparsely tied streamer is a super fly for taking fish that have forsaken insects.

Golden Demon. The New England version of the Golden Demon fly has proven to be far more effective than its western counterpart. As a trout fly it is perhaps one of the top flies for both casting and trolling.

Silver Demon. Basically the same as the Golden Demon, this fly is also an excellent one to cast or troll for trout.

T-Bone. This versatile fly has proven to be effective everywhere. It resembles the Little Woody, but has brown hen hackle tied palmer over its body. It's a must for every serious angler.

Kerplunk Fly. This weighted fly originated by Joe Blazonis is an excellent fly for rainbow and brook trout. It is wire-bodied and can be cast or trolled.

Wooly Bugger. This popular fly is perhaps one of the best for trout that is readily available. Tied thickly Palmer-style with the forward hackle tied back makes it even more enticing.

In the chapter on trolling, we will discuss streamers. Before going further, I wish to single out one fly in particular, the Hornberg. It is perhaps the all-time favorite of New England sportsman and it has proven to be effective everywhere trout can be found. I have found over the years that the original Hornberg pattern, though excellent, can often be enhanced by varying the color. Varying the wing color with brown, green, or yellow will entice trout to strike. A flash of red under the outer wings makes the fly deadly. We will discuss the Hornberg more fully in Chapter 2.

Other flies that have proven their worth in the United States and around the world are the Coachman, the Royal Coachman, the Cowdung, the Parmechene Belle, and the March Brown. These are described in almost every book on flies written in the past decade, so their dressings will not be described here.

DRESSINGS FOR FLY PATTERNS

BLACK GNAT
Hook sizes:	#14 to #20 Black
Head:	Black
Tail:	Three black hackle fibers
Body:	Black chenille (fine)
Throat:	Small bunch of black hackle fibers
Wing:	Black dyed duck or slate gray duck wing feathers, short clipped. This is optional, since in smaller sizes wings are not needed

CLAIRE'S CREEPER
Hook sizes:	#12, 2x1
Tail:	Black bear hair tied so that it extends front and rear about one-quarter inch
Body:	Black floss painted over with several coats of black lacquer

DAN'S LEECH
Hook size:	#8 or 10
Head:	Black
Body:	Black ostrich herl (four strands)
Ribbing:	Small flat silver tinsel
Tail:	Black marabou (one half inch)

ED'S FLY
Hook size:	#10
Head:	Black
Tail:	Brown hen hackle, fibers (sparse)
Body:	Black wool, built up heavy
Throat:	Brown hen hackle fibers
Wing:	Wood duck breast feather

HERON FLY
Hook size:	#10
Head:	Brown
Body:	Olive wool
Ribbing:	Olive hackle tied palmer
Wing:	Wood duck (cut a V out of the feather and lay it flat on top)

HOUSE FLY

Hook sizes:	#10 to #14
Head:	Black
Body:	Black Ostrich herl
Throat:	Small bunch of black saddle hackle fibers (sparse)
Wing:	Guinea hen hackle

LAMMA

Hook sizes:	#10, #12
Head:	Black
Body:	Claret red floss (green floss optional pattern)
Ribbing:	Medium flat silver tinsel
Hackle:	Barred Plymouth Rock hackle tied completely around
Wing:	Squirrel tail (white tipped with a little black)

LITTLE DEVIL

Hook size:	#10, 3x1
Head:	Black Ostrich herl
Tail:	Red wool
Body:	Medium flat silver tinsel
Wing:	Dark turkey over gray squirrel tail

LITTLE WOODY

Hook sizes:	#8 to #16
Head:	Black
Tail:	Three to four strands, brown hen hackle fibers
Body:	Peacock herl
Throat:	Small bunch of brown hen hackles
Wing:	Wood duck, sparsely tied
Variation:	Tail and throat, red hackle fibers (Female)

MINK FLY

Hook size:	#16
Head:	Black
Body:	Peacock herl
Wing:	Mink fur

PEACOCK FLY

Hook size:	#10, 3x1
Head:	Black
Body:	Peacock herl
Ribbing:	Medium flat silver tinsel
Wing:	Wood duck breast feather

PEACOCK NYMPH
Hook size:	#14 to #18, wet
Body:	Peacock herl eye, stripped bare
Head:	Black Ostrich herl

GOLDEN DEMON FLY
Hook size:	#8 or 10
Head:	Black
Tail:	One golden pheasant tippet
Body:	Gold holographic Mylar tinsel, medium or size 14, (plain gold optional)
Throat:	Small bunch of orange hackles
Wing:	Bronzed mallard, sparse, topped with gold Krystal Flash or pearlescent Flashabou

SILVER DEMON FLY   (Substitute gold above with silver Mylar tinsel)

RED HEAD
Hook size:	#10, #12, 4xl
Head:	Red
Body:	Medium flat silver tinsel
Ribbing:	Oval silver tinsel
Wing:	Red squirrel tail over a few strands of white impala tail tied sparse

T-BONE
Hook size:	#6 to #10, 2xl
Head:	Black
Tail:	Three to four strands, brown hen hackle fibers
Body:	Peacock herl
Ribbing:	Brown hen hackle tied palmer, then snipped short (optional medium, flat silver or gold tinsel, with brown hackle wrapped over and snipped short)
Throat:	Small bunch of brown hen hackle fibers
Wing:	Wood duck

KERPLUNK
Hook size:	#6 to #10, 2xl
Head:	Black
Tail:	Strands of black hackle
Body:	Black wire
Throat:	Black hackle wound several times at the head
Wing:	Two to three strands silver Mylar Flashabou

WOOLY BUGGER

Hook size:	#8 to #10
Head:	Black
Tail:	Black marabou
Body:	Black chenille
Hackle:	Black, palmered to front and tied back at the head

COACHMAN VARIATION

Hook size:	#8 to #16
Head:	Black
Tail:	Red
Body:	Peacock herl
Throat:	Red or brown hackle fibers (color optional)
Wing:	White or gray rabbit fur (color optional)

This simple fly works well with a white or gray wing of rabbit guard hairs. Rabbit fur has a tantalizing effect when drawn through water that drives trout wild.

FLY FISHING TACKLE AND TECHNIQUES

An array of fishing flies will not serve you well unless you have the means to deliver them. This is usually done with a well-balanced fly rod combination. I will also discuss other methods of delivering a fly, but first, let's discuss the basic fly rod outfit.

In fly-fishing the rod must be matched to the line in order to deliver the fly. The reel is probably the least important piece of equipment. It should be sturdy with a smooth action, and large enough to hold the fly line and perhaps fifty to one hundred yards of backing material, such as monofilament line or better yet, some multifilament medium such as Dacron or nylon line. The fly line and backing material should be joined with a nail knot for smooth movement through the guides should there be a need.

Two of the best fly reels are the Pflueger Medalist reels in all of their various sizes, and the Shakespeare reels. Both reels are inexpensive and trustworthy.

They each offer interchangeability of spools, so that you can carry several types of fly line without having to purchase additional reels. For fly-casting, the Pflueger Medalist 1495 and 1495 1/2 are perhaps the best reels.

For fishermen who are going astream with just one fly rod, the best all-round fly rod is an eight-foot fiberglass or a nine-foot graphite, medium-action rod. These will accommodate number five and six weight lines. They are ideal for trout, panfish, and even bass.

Fly lines are at the heart of fly-fishing. Unless the line is properly matched to the rod, casting can become a chore, and a fruitless one at that. Most manufacturers rate their rods for certain fly line weights at the factory. These recommended weights are fairly exact and should be followed.

To properly fish a fly, you should have four different fly lines. I must confess that I prefer the weight-forward lines, which simply means they are shaped so that the forward section of the line, a few feet behind the tip end, is heavier than the body of the line. This forward weight allows for easier casting and most important, it will allow you to cast under windy conditions. The drawback is that when presenting a dry fly, it will not land as softly as a tapered fly line sans the extra weight.

Because the dry fly season is relatively short and I do not propose to be a dry fly purist or expert, let's stay with the methods that work best. The following fly lines will enable you to fish under all prevailing conditions.

Dry Line. This line will allow you to fish with a dry fly, or present a fly just under the surface. In ponds and lakes, trout usually feed on emerging insects just beneath the surface.

Sinking-tip Line. This line will allow you to fish close to the top since the first five to ten feet only will sink. The body of the line will float.

Sinking Fly Line. This line will allow you to fish deeper and is useful on lakes and ponds when the fish are down. It descends slowly and you have to allow time for it to sink. Sinking lines can be purchased to sink to various depths, but the average sinking line will work at approximately ten feet while being retrieved.

Super-fast-Sinking Fly Line. This line is very useful especially in the spring and when trolling is desirable. It has a high density and will sink rapidly. When being retrieved it will work at approximately twenty feet, making it ideal for pond fishing.

Leaders are in a class all by themselves. Expert fly fishermen can throw a fly line with a twelve to sixteen-foot leader without difficulty. There is seldom if any need for us hackers to do this. When this need arises, there are other ways we can entice fish.

Most leaders need only be seven to nine feet long to take fish. I have fished with leaders as short as three feet. Not because I cannot cast a longer leader, but because there are times when a short leader will bring the fly closer to the bottom so that I can dredge the fly along the bed of a pond.

I prefer the knotless leaders, such as those made by the Berkley Company. After experimenting with my own leaders, suiting them to what I thought were my needs, I finally decided that commercial leaders are as good, if not much better. Wind knots in leaders are something we try to avoid while casting. Why, then, tie leaders and add half a dozen knots intentionally?

I carry along a leader packet with seven-foot and nine-foot leaders in a wide array of tippet weights. These leaders will range from a one-pound tippet to five pounds. The most serviceable tippet for trout fishing is three pounds.

For those days when the trout become especially selective and I have cut back my tippet to the point where the leader is no longer useful, I carry a spool of nylon monofilament sewing thread. This relatively inexpensive material is rated at about one pound test and a single spool will last for several seasons. It is a simple matter to tie on three feet of this material and continue fishing without changing the entire leader.

Deciding how and when to use the fly rod for trout is a question that puzzles most part-time fly rod users. Purists naturally have no trouble with this issue since they use it at all times. But woe to those of us who tend to fish with bait and lure for most of the year.

The best thing to do is to take along your fly rod and a box of flies whenever you go out. You never know for certain when the fish may be dimpling on the surface, or when they may be taking some aquatic insect. A good fisherman should be prepared for all the possibilities at all times.

If you have become adept at fly casting, then you already know that anytime the fish are willing, you can take them with the right fly. The flies described in this chapter are all that you will need to enjoy our sport. Presenting them is another matter, and because that subject has been described in books and pamphlets by the hundreds, I won't bore you with it. I'll simply give you a few tips on the casting aspects that I have found to be effective over the years.

Don't cast on top of a rise. Take a few seconds to watch how a fish is working and then lead it with the fly. If it is feeding on the surface or just beneath it, chances are the fish will be spooky. Unless, of course, it is a freshly stocked trout, in which case it may not matter. But try to lead the fish, and try especially to lay the fly down as gently as possible. Let it set for a moment and then begin with a slow retrieve. If this doesn't work, quicken the pace of the retrieve.

I find it best to hold the fly line between the handle and my right forefinger and strip it in with my left hand. The overhand retrieve is too awkward under most fishing conditions.

Many fly rod purists keep the rod up at a slight angle. I prefer to keep it parallel to the water and watch the line, or judge by feel when a trout takes the fly. I then sweep the rod upwards sharply to set the hook. In this way, the rod will absorb the shock of the strike before the fish decides to make a run for it.

For fish that are deep, I follow the same method as for those feeding near the surface. The difference is that when using a super-fast-sinking line, my retrieves are almost always quick. And when fishing deep, it is important to be aware of the line between your fingers, because the combination of fish and hasty retrieve will undoubtedly telegraph through feel, much as in bait fishing.

To give a fly such as the Red Head some action, I will often raise the rod to about a forty-five degree angle and shake the rod while retrieving briskly. This causes the fly to dance upon the retrieve. It has enticed many a reluctant trout. Best of all, this technique is not restricted to the use of that one fly, but works with many other wet flies and streamers. It is an especially effective retrieve when employing the roll cast.

A very productive technique in a boat is to simply drift with the fly behind the boat. This is especially effective when the fish are near the surface. If they are down deep, use a sinking line, row slowly, and keep a sharp eye on the line. Any unusual movement should by all means be construed as a fish. There is no room for doubters in the sport of fishing.

There are a few things that you can do to make your fly-fishing more comfortable and for that matter much more efficient. So much so that you will often take fish while other fisherman go empty.

You can start by carrying some of the flies described in this chapter in a convenient fly box. I like those boxes that have clips on the cover to hold the larger flies, and compartments to hold the smaller ones. Two boxes should be more than enough to hold the flies you will need under most fishing conditions. With eight compartments each, you can carry a wide range of assorted flies in each box. Place the flies in the boxes so that one holds your dark patterns and the other your bright and standard patterns. This will save you time in searching for the right fly. Change flies often, but not constantly. Give each fly a fair chance.

Too many fishermen spend their fly-fishing time trying to find the right fly, when all they need to do is try it at different depths or use a different retrieve. About thirty to forty-five minutes per fly will prove its worth.

Wear a fly-fishing vest, and carry in it the necessities of the sport: a small nail clip, hook hone, fly line dressing, leader-sink material, a wallet type leader packet, a piece of rubber inner-tube attached via a chain snap to straighten out curled leaders, and a small flashlight. A new light is now being marketed that is relatively inexpensive and handy. It is a flashlight that turns on when you bite it, thus freeing your hands for tying a fly.

I modify my fishing vests and even my shirts for that matter. The first thing I do is to attach grommets to the pocket flaps. These grommet holes are just large enough to accommodate a chain snap. In this way, I can conveniently hang many of the small tools that I will need while fishing. I don't have to search for an item in one of the many pockets of the vest each time I need something.

The trend today is to use small fancy-looking landing nets. These are elongated in shape and appear "classy." They are just fine for the fisherman who does not feel optimistic enough to ever believe he will catch large trout. If he does, he will have much more difficulty netting the fish than he did while playing it with the fly rod.

I use a large net. Actually, my wading net is a small boat net with a frame approximately sixteen inches across and twenty-four inches long. The handle is cut to about two feet in length. I then place a dowel or piece of broom handle down the shaft of the handle for strength and wrap the handle with a heavy-duty thread for a handgrip. I finish it with a rod butt cap into which I insert a screw eye with a French snap attached.

With such a net I can land any trout, bass, or shad, in these parts. I don't have to flounder about at that critical moment when a large fish is making its final desperate surge for freedom. And it is not cumbersome to carry on the D-ring that is attached to the back of a fishing vest.

I also add a piece of reflective material to my landing net toward the net end. This affords me better vision when evening fishing, or when shad fishing if I am using a headlamp. I also add an elastic band to the handle to keep the net from hanging while walking. The net should be freed prior to fishing however, so that you won't have to fumble with it when time is critical.

Always wear a belt around the outside of waders to avoid serious injury should you fall. A belt snug around the waist will buy you enough time to recover your footing before too much water enters over the top. A belt is not foolproof, so caution should always be used while wading. Today, there is a fine wader belt made with a quick release much like that of car safety belts. For fewer than six dollars, it is a fine investment.

I often use a wading staff when I am fishing a strange pond or lake, especially when fishing murky water or water that is deceptively clear. Wading staffs can be purchased for twenty dollars or you can make your own. A ski pole with the basket removed will do just fine. Ski poles have a fine handgrip, are sturdy, and can be usually obtained free from some ski buff friend.

When it comes to methods of storing captured fish, I often use a creel. I have found the best creels are the Arctic type with pockets. The pockets are useful for keeping bait or flies handy.

When fishing from a boat I use a very large net. There is no reason to lose a fish because of a net too small for the job. A wide, deep, long-handled net will afford you the opportunity to land a fish with little effort and less movement.

For boat fishing, a small fishing bag, such as those sold by the Orvis Company or Eddie Bauer, will enable you to carry a great deal of fishing tackle along and keep it out of harm's way. With six to seven compartments, it offers room for fly boxes, reels, and a host of items you will need.

During the spring months, stringing captured trout is fine. As the weather warms, I prefer to store them in a cooler with ice. Fish spoil easily, and because a boat offers the luxury of room to store a cooler it is wise to do so.

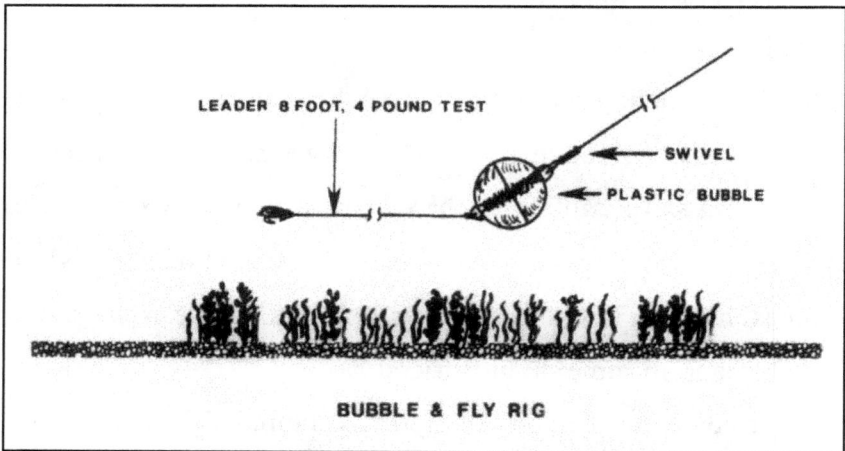

LEADER 8 FOOT, 4 POUND TEST

SWIVEL

PLASTIC BUBBLE

BUBBLE & FLY RIG

Fly Fishing With A Bubble

Not everyone is inclined to fish with a fly rod. Even those of us who are inclined to do so find that there are times when weather conditions, ability, or equipment hinder us in our efforts. I can remember many times when I would see fish rising just out of range of my ability to cast to them. Those are frustrating moments, since I knew that all it would take to catch a few would be to get the fly within their sphere.

Nowadays, I always carry a spinning rod along even when I go fly-fishing. On "Fly Fishing Only" ponds, of course, this is not legal and should be avoided. But on the majority of ponds and lakes, the bubble can and often does save the day. In over thirty-five years of bubble fishing, I have had many reasons to thank the anonymous individual who concocted the idea. Another candidate for the Fishing Hall of Fame perhaps.

To use the bubble and fly combination properly, I use an eight-foot rod, but the combination can be used with a seven-foot rod as well. My bubble rod is an eight-foot fly rod blank constructed as a spinning rod. With this extra length, I can fish an eight-foot long leader with the fly. The extra length allows me to execute a smooth back cast without the fly hitting the water. I can also cast further and more accurately. Most important, the hooking power is awesome. The light tip allows me to retrieve trout that are lightly hooked as well as those that have bought the steel.

All of the favorite flies used with a fly rod can be used with the bubble, although small wet flies are best. When fishing just under the surface, the Black Gnat, Little Woody, and T-Bone are excellent. When fishing down deep, Dan's Leech, the Golden Demon and Claire's Creeper are all deadly.

The bubble is simply a hollow plastic ball with a spring device that can be squeezed to allow water to enter. This is to allow the fisherman to add weight to the bubble. What I do is keep some of the bubbles as they are. With others I add small pieces of lead.

I use the plain bubbles to fish the surface, and the weighted bubbles to fish just below the surface or down deep. Adding water to the lead-laden bubble will make them sink to the bottom when the trout are deep.

A straight three-pound test leader is all that is necessary. There is really no need to use a tapered leader. Once the fly is cast, a few turns of the reel handle will straighten out the leader. If on the surface; let it set a moment, then retrieve slowly. When fishing deep, allow enough time to let the bubble sink, counting if necessary, and then begin a slow retrieve. With the bubble, slow is more effective than fast while retrieving.

I have been tying my own flies for over forty years now, and despite this fact, I have resisted becoming a purist. Perhaps some of you readers will one day become so addicted to this fine aspect of angling that you may well become another Lee Wulff.

If you decide at the outset to simply try to catch fish, then the tips I have just offered will enable you to catch them often. I have been employing these techniques since my youth, and they work.

When fly fishing, always be willing to be innovative or creative. Don't be afraid to cut the wing from a fly to make it look like a nymph if necessary. Many times I have altered a fly while astream only to find that it proved to be the difference between a limit and no fish at all. Any fly with a peacock herl body is a good example. The buggy-looking peacock herl is always attractive to trout, with or without a wing and tail.

Lead-core trolling reels. Left back: Shakespeare wide spool multiplier reel; 2:1 gear ratio. Right back: Shakespeare narrow spool multiplier reel: 2:1 gear ratio. Left front: Minot 109; 3:1 gear ratio. Right front: Pflueger 1495; 1:1 gear ratio. Multiplier reels, with their quick retrieve capabilities, are best for trolling.

2

Trolling for Trout

One of the most effective ways to catch trout in any season is by trolling. Not with a spinner and worm, or even with lures, but with flies.

Although trolled bait and hardware attract a great many fish, brown rainbow, and brook trout each will succumb to a small streamer fly dragged behind a boat.

To troll successfully for trout, I use lead-core line. There are times when a super-fast-sinking fly line will work just as well, but lead-core line is by far the most consistent medium to bring the fly down deep. Whenever lead-core line is mentioned, fishermen conjure up visions of heavyweight tackle: the type used on huge lakes when seeking lake trout. This image could not be further from the truth. Trolling for trout with lead-core line is an effective way to take trout in small ponds as well as in large lakes. In fact, lead-core line is well suited to ponds and small lakes because trolling with this weighted line will enable you to find the fish no matter what the depth, and at the same time, to discover the hazards of a lake or pond's structure.

With lead-core line you will soon learn where the weedy areas and the shoals are located. You'll learn these things the hard way, cussing as you leave behind a streamer stuck on some unseen obstacle lurking below.

For all the frustration that a new troller may encounter in getting used to lead-core line fishing, it will be well worth the effort in the end. Fortunately it is not too difficult to learn how to fish with lead-core line. And the tackle is so light and sporty that you will enjoy catching fish. A caveat is in order though. The deeper you must fish to catch a trout the less enjoyable it becomes. But then, this is almost always the case with the various techniques we employ.

For starters and before we get into the meat of lead-core lines, please do one thing. Promise yourself that you'll think positive. This chapter may introduce you to the most productive fishing method you will ever learn in your entire life.

I could not begin to describe the number of fish that I have captured over the years with lead-core line, without sounding as though I were telling tall tales in true fisherman's fashion. But over the years I have taken enough fish to make any angler happy beyond his dreams. Furthermore, many of these successful outings were on days when other fishermen went home empty.

I always fish a new trout pond or lake with lead-core line. After I have thus found the fish, I look for other methods. But usually, the old lead-core line trick is the one that works best, especially when the going gets tough during the warm months. Lead-core line trolling is perhaps the ultimate method for all seasons. You will rarely fail to conjure up a fish or two with this method.

TACKLE

You don't need heavy equipment to troll with lead-core line. In fact, heavy equipment will cause you to tire quickly and take the joy out of fishing. Let's discuss the tackle needed to successfully troll for trout with lead-core line.

Rod. An eight-foot, medium-action fly rod is all that you will need to handle most lead-line situations. In most bodies of water where you encounter trout, the water depth is such that five to six colors are usually the maximum you'll need to fish. If you have to use more than six colors, the best bet is to go to wire line.

I have tried many fly rods over the years while trolling for trout with lead-core line and a medium-action rod works best. It has enough backbone to bear up under the weight of the line and to allow you to set the hook when the rod bends sharply under the weight of a fish.

Stiff, heavy rods will not allow you to set the hook better, or reach the fish to a greater degree. They will, as stated earlier, cause you to tire more quickly. Lead-core line fishing requires a great deal of effort that is borne by the forearm and wrist.

Reels. Years ago multiplier reels were easily obtained. These reels are excellent for trolling because you can retrieve line at a ratio of two to one. This made both paying out line and retrieving it much easier. This seemingly small advantage can loom big when, if you play a fish off the spool as I do, you want to keep the line taut under windy conditions.

Now days most multiplier reels have been discontinued. What few are available are very expensive. The least expensive is made by the Martin Reel Company out of New York, but it is not as smooth as those formerly sold by Shakespeare, L.L. Bean and Orvis. The cost of a Martin multiplier reel is around one hundred dollars.

I kept the picture of these reels in this book so that you might recognize them should you see them at a yard sale or flea market. Probably the only places you will ever find them again.

While my preference is to use multiplier reels, single action reels do work well for lead-core line fishing. Pflueger Medallist reels are fine and inexpensive and the 1495 ½ model is large enough to hold at least eight colors of line. But if you get serious about trolling with lead-core line, a reel with a good disc drag is very helpful. This is because when you are trolling, you never know how big a fish you may hook into.

Line.   Years ago they made some lead-core line with a plastic outer coating. This line was exceptional because it was easy on the rod guides and was kind to the fingers. Because lead-core line is not exactly a best seller, and has great longevity, the company stopped producing it. Now day's lead-core line is made with nylon coating. It is strong and will last many years. But it is not as gentle to the rod guides or fingers as the old plastic coated line.

Lead-core line is color coded so that fisherman can know how much line is paid out. It changes color every ten yards for the first five colors then the colors repeat. This repetition is good for fishermen because with the exception of some very large, deep lakes, fishermen only need to fill their reels with five colors or one hundred and fifty feet of lead-core line. Since lead-core line comes in one hundred-yard spools, two reels may be filled, or the extra line can be saved for such time as the motors propeller severs the line while fishing. This is something that happens to all trollers eventually.

Line weight for lead-core line should not exceed eighteen-pound test. It is not the lead core line that comes into contact with the fish so don't feel that such a heavy line weight is unsporting. Through the years I have found this line weight to be more than adequate for all freshwater fishing. Heavier lines add weight to a reel and because they are slightly larger in diameter they result in a bigger belly in the line while trolling.

All fishermen who use lead-core line will catch the bottom once in a while but most often it is the leader that will be lost as a result of a hang up and not the lead-core line. I usually use twenty-feet of six-pound test monofilament between my lead-core line and the fly. The leader is attached to the tag end of the lead-core line via a needle knot. Six-pound test monofilament is strong enough to absorb the shock of a strike and small enough not to bother leader shy fish.

There will be times when it might be wise to reduce the length of the leader while fishing with lead-core line. One such time is when you are using a lure such as a Super Duper. Another is when you feel an absolute need to keep the leader short because you want to get down a bit deeper with less line played out. However, a shortened leader will change the action of the fly.

While it appears that most fish will smash a fly with gusto as soon as they see it, I have had fish follow a fly some distance before actually striking it. This is usually made known by slight taps as the fish nips at the fly prior to striking it hard enough to become hooked. Fish often hook themselves when they strike a trolled fly or lure, but it is wise to strike them back when you feel the hit to assure that the barb of the hook penetrates deeply.

HOW TO FISH WITH LEAD-CORE LINE

To properly fish with lead-core line you should begin by doing your homework where it is most comfortable: at home. While you may be able to fish a new pond cold turkey and be successful, I have found that knowing a bit about the depth and structure of a pond cuts my search time considerably. This homework is achieved by gathering maps of ponds and lakes from a variety of sources. Check the Internet for possible sources and also check with the nearest Division of Fisheries and Wildlife if you reside in the U.S. Many overseas governments also have similarly named agencies. Commercial map books are also in print. Because they can be a bit pricey, they are the last resort.

Lead-core line sinks about four to six feet per ten yards, so it helps to know the depth of a pond. If you are going to fish a small pond, with depths below thirty feet or so, you will know that it is safe to fish at four colors. At this depth, you will find fish lurking near the bottom. To pay out more than four colors will result in dressing your fly with weeds and hanging up on debris at the bottom.

A good way to start with lead-core line is to fish deep and work up. Over the years, this method has worked best. Starting at the top and working down seems logical, but the most effective way is from the bottom up. I don't know the scientific explanation for this; it just seems to work.

Patterning will enable you to cover a pond thoroughly. When I first fish a body of water in search of trout, I skirt the edges. If this fails to yield a trout, I begin to skirt the pond further from the shore. As a last resort, I zigzag the pond much as a hunting dog quarters a field. In this way, I not only cover the entire pond, but I also cover various depths because the lead-core line will rise on the straight runs and drop during the turns.

So before you begin to go astream, learn as much about a body of water as you can. Bring a spare copy of a map with you and mark it. In short order, you will have a complete file on the pond and be able to find fish quickly and consistently.

An electronic fish-finder is a useful tool to use while trolling with lead-core line. It will not help you to catch fish, however. I have found that most fish spotted on the screen have simply passed through the cone-shaped signal or else I simply passed over them. In many instances, fish spotted on the dial may not be trout, but panfish. Using an electronic fish-finder while trolling, then, is for a purpose other than spying on fish. Its function is to find the bottom of the pond and to keep track of its variations.

When the fish-finder is registering thirty-feet, you know that you can safely fish four to five colors of line. Depending upon speed, lead-core line will sink approximately four to six feet per color. If you are trolling ever so slowly, the line will sink deeper. If you are trolling at a fast pace, the line will rise. At a moderate speed, four colors of line will descend to about twenty-four feet.

If, for example, you are trolling at a moderate speed with four colors of lead-core line out behind your boat and the fish-finder begins to indicate that the contour of the pond's bottom is changing from deep to shallow, then you must retrieve line so that you will keep your fly at a desirable depth. If you don't you will have to cleanse the hook of weeds. Should the fish-finder indicate that the water is deepening, you can let out an additional color or two.

The electronic fish-finder is a useful tool for several other reasons. It is a good navigational aid and it will also help you to chart those ponds or lakes for which you have not been able to locate a map. With a fish-finder you may accurately record the structure of a pond as well as its depth. Fish-finders will distinguish, by variations in signals on the screen, muck from rock and also weedy areas.

Another tool that I have used successfully over the years is a Trollex. This is a useful device for registering the speed of a boat while trolling. Basically, the Trollex is a plastic dial with numbers registering up to the digit eight. A one-ounce lead weight is attached to a fifteen-inch length of monofilament line affixed to the bottom of a lever. The Trollex itself is clamped to the gunnel of the boat. The sinker is dropped over the side so that it is approximately eight inches under the water. As the boat moves, the sinker drags and causes the lever to move. In this way, it is easy to find out if a certain speed is being maintained.

The Trollex is not an accurate speedometer, but it was not designed for that purpose. It simply lets a fisherman know that if he is trolling with the wind to his back and he is reading a "four" on the Trollex, then when he then faces the wind, he should maintain a four reading on the meter. Several other speed-monitoring devices are available today, all of which will work to aid you in maintaining a constant speed.

Maintaining the proper speed while trolling becomes especially important once a trout or two are caught. If, for example, you took two rainbows at three colors down chances are you will catch more fish at that exact same depth. If you are fishing in the wind, and many of our days are spent that way, the Trollex becomes invaluable in maintaining the correct speed no matter what the direction of the boat with respect to the wind.

High speed is not conducive to good trolling for trout. I like to maintain a speed that will enable me to pay the line down to the depths, but at the same time allow me to control my rod. Whenever I troll with flies, I continuously sweep the rod in a back-and-forth motion. Over the years, this sweeping action has proven to be most effective. And the sweeps are not gentle ones, but vigorous ones that bring the fly upward in a darting motion. It is usually on the downward drop that trout take the fly. It is when you once again sweep forward that you feel the strike, and it feels as though you have hung on the bottom of the pond. That is a heady feeling, to say the least.

Another excellent method to impart action to the fly while trolling is to place the tip end of the fly rod into the water and to grasp the line working only the line back and forth. With the rod tip in the water there is less effort required in applying action to the fly. The drawback is that you will not feel the strike with the same gusto as when the rod is out of the water.

Once a trout has struck the fly it is important not to allow any slack line. To prevent the fish from using the line to advantage by utilizing the weight of the lead-core line for leverage, do the following: Keep the boat moving just long enough to reel in enough line to assure that you can feel the fish. Your rod will be arched and the lead line should be straight out with no slack appearing. Next, shut the motor or place it in neutral and begin retrieving.

With a two-to-one action reel, there will be little slack line present during the retrieve. With a single action reel you will have to work a bit faster to retrieve line quickly. Once you can see the leader, or you are but one color out from the rod tip, be prepared. When the bulk of the lead-core line is spooled the trout will usually make its strongest bid for freedom. Be ready and willing to give it line. Trout taken on lead-core line are not pushovers dazed by sudden shock from water temperature changes. They fight and fight hard.

I use a rod holder on occasion, but only when the fishing is difficult. On days when presenting flies of differing patterns may help to locate trout, I place one rod in a rod holder. Although the stationary rod will take fish, more are lost because the rod is not being hand held. It is important whenever using lead-core line to strike back when a fish takes the fly, and to strike back hard. Lead-core line tends to form a belly that has to be accounted for if the hook is to sink deeply into the trout's jaw

Another device that works well when using one rod is a dropper fly. This fly should be a different color than the one on the terminal end of the leader. A light fly and a dark fly make a good combination. Although you may occasionally hook a double, the main purpose of the dropper fly combination is simply to find out whether the trout prefer a dark or a light pattern.

On fly fishing only lakes; it is often illegal to use lead-core line. In order to troll deep there are several methods that can be employed. One is to use what is known as salmon sinking line; this is a heavy, level line that will get down deeply. Another method is to splice two super fast sinking fly lines together.

To splice two fly lines together scrape about one inch of the line coating from each line. Do this at the tag end of what is to be the front line and at the tip end of the second rearmost line. Bond the two lines together with Super Glue, then wrap the two with fly tying thread. Finally coat the whole joint with rubberized bonding cement. I paint the bond bright red so that I can tell when I am at the joint, which is always the weakest link of the line.

This fly line will enable you to legally fish in any venue where use of lead-core line is restricted.

FLIES FOR TROLLING
WITH LEAD-CORE LINE

There are so many patterns of streamer flies that a fisherman might think it almost impossible to select the right one to catch trout. And if that weren't bad enough, many ponds have reputations for being suitable only for particular fly patterns. Tales abound of how Joe Jones takes his limit with a left-winged dingbat fly while other anglers gawk in empty-handed awe.

The truth is that over the years, there have been a few instances in which I have had to change my fly pattern to meet a certain need. But these instances have been rare. For the most part, the flies I am about to discuss will take fish in all trout ponds at least 95 percent of the time. That is not simply a fancy statement but a matter of fact. As you fish with lead-core line and try the patterns tied as described in these pages you will become a believer.

I hold to the theory that color is of the utmost importance in lead-core line fishing. I know that a two-punch system has worked for me over the years. I use streamers of every color during the daylight hours. But at dusk, I always use bright colors. Yellow and white-winged streamers will attract trout during those periods when dusk is quickly descending on a pond. This technique has brought that extra trout or two to net at the shank end of a day too often to be a coincidence.

Streamers for trout fishing with lead-core line need not be large. Some anglers I have known over the years contended that they would not fish with anything but a size eight streamer or larger. Their reasoning, oddly enough, was that they wanted a fly that the trout could see. I won't argue with anyone who thinks this way. I'll simply state that when fishing with some of these anglers, I have out-fished them with my smaller streamers to the point that some have conceded that large is not the way to go when tying or buying streamer flies for trout. Unless you know for certain that the fish you are going to catch consistently are in the jumbo class, you should be using small streamers.

I tie my streamers on size 8, 10, and 12 hooks one-half inch longer than regular shanked hooks. These sizes are large enough to attract and catch the largest of fish in these parts. Use only the finest hooks, such as Mustad, Eagle Claw, or Daiichi and you will land large fish with no fear of loss through hooks straightening out.

The New England version of the Golden Demon is perhaps one of the all-time great trout flies ever created. For lead-core line trolling, its reputation is assured. I use several variations of this streamer fly; all tied no larger than a size eight. These variations do not change the fly so much that it cannot be recognized as a Golden Demon.

Dan's Leech and the Wooly Bugger are two other favorite trolling flies that I have used extensively over the past two decades. These excellent flies add to my arsenal of the Gray Ghost streamer and its variations; the Pink Ghost, Black Ghost, and the Green Ghost. All are excellent trolling streamers for trout.

I do strip the original ghost patterns of some of their fancy trappings, however. I omit the peacock herl and golden pheasant crest. I also tie the streamers sparse. To allow for my theory of light and dark colors with respect to daylight or dusk fishing, I vary the throat, which extends the length of the fly, by using either all white or all yellow impala tail.

Other flies that I prefer are the Colonel Bates, an excellent bright yellow streamer, the Hornberg tied in a variety of colors, and the light and dark Edson Tigers. The Dark Edson Tiger is varied by simply winging it with a white wing instead of yellow.

I have found the T-Bone fly, described in Chapter 1, excellent for trolling, even though it is not a streamer.

Streamer Fly Patterns

BLACK GHOST

Hook sizes:	#8, 10, and 12, ½ inch longer shank
Tail:	Yellow hackle fibers
Body:	Black floss
Ribbing:	Flat medium silver tinsel
Throat:	Yellow hackle fibers
Wing:	Four white streamer hackles
Cheek:	Jungle cock

COLONEL BATES

Hook sizes:	#8, 10, and 12, ½ inch longer shank
Head:	Black with red collar
Tail:	Red hackle fibers or duck wing quill
Body:	Flat medium silver tinsel
Wing:	Two white streamer hackles over which are placed two yellow streamer hackles. Opposite the original pattern.
Throat:	Small bunch of brown hen fibers
Cheek:	Teal or wood duck breast feathers

DARK EDSON TIGER

Hook sizes:	#8, 10, and 12, 4xl
Head:	Yellow
Tail:	Yellow hackle fibers
Body:	Yellow chenille
Throat:	Red hackle fibers
Cheek:	Jungle cock (optional)

GARRISON GASSER

Hook sizes:	#8, 10 and 12, ½ inch longer shank
Head:	Black
Body:	Medium flat, embossed silver tinsel
Throat:	Brown hackle fibers
Wing:	Brown hackles from a yellow dyed bucktail, sparse
Cheek:	Jungle cock (optional)

GRAY GHOST

Hook sizes:	#8, 10, and 12, ½ inch longer shank
Head:	Black
Body:	Orange floss
Ribbing:	Flat medium silver tinsel
Throat:	White or yellow impala, sparse
Wing:	Four gray streamer hackles
Cheeks:	Silver pheasant with jungle cock (optional)

GREEN GHOST

Hook sizes:	#8, 10, and 12, ½ inch longer shank
Body:	Orange floss
Ribbing:	Flat medium silver tinsel
Throat:	White or yellow impala
Wing:	Four green streamer hackles
Cheeks:	Silver pheasant with jungle cock (optional)

LIGHT EDSON TIGER

Hook sizes:	#8 10, and 12, 4xl
Head:	Black
Tail:	Silver pheasant fibers
Body:	Peacock herl
Wing:	White or yellow impala
Shoulder:	Small bunch of duck quill placed on top of wing
Cheek:	Jungle cock (optional)

NINE-THREE

Hook sizes:	#8, 10, and 12, ½ inch longer shank
Head:	Black
Body:	Flat medium silver tinsel
Ribbing:	Small oval silver tinsel
Throat:	White impala
Wing:	Two green under two black streamer hackles
Cheeks:	Jungle cock (optional)

PINK GHOST

Hook sizes:	#8, 10, and 12, ½ inch longer shank
Body:	Pink floss
Ribbing:	Flat medium gold tinsel
Throat:	White impala, sparse
Wing:	Four pink streamer hackles
Cheeks:	Silver pheasant with jungle cock (optional)

SUPERVISOR

Hook sizes:	#8, 10, and 12, ½ inch longer shank
Head:	Black
Tail:	Red wool, or red hackle fibers
Body:	Flat medium silver tinsel
Ribbing:	Small oval silver tinsel
Throat:	White impala
Wing:	Small bunch of impala over which are tied four light blue streamer hackles, topped with three strands of peacock herl
Cheeks:	Jungle cock (optional)

WOOD DUCK

Hook sizes:	#8, 10, 12 4xl
Head:	Black
Tail:	Wood duck fibers
Body:	Peacock herl
Ribbing:	Optional. Medium silver or gold flat tinsel
Throat:	Brown hen fibers
Wing:	Wood duck breast feather

WOOLY WORM

Hook sizes:	#8, 10, 12, ½ inch longer shank
Head:	Black
Tail:	Brown hen hackle fibers
Body:	Peacock herl
Ribbing:	Brown hen hackles tied Palmer

HORNBERGS

The Hornberg is a productive fly pattern tied with so many variations that it would not suffice to simply describe its most noted dressing. The following pattern will present the Hornberg in its original form, but to truly appreciate the value of this fly, we will discuss its many variations, all of which will catch trout at one time or another.

HORNBERG

Hook sizes:	#8, 10, and 12, 3xl
Head:	Black
Body:	Medium flat silver tinsel
Wing:	Underwing sparse yellow hackle fibers, over which are placed mallard feathers tied one to a side.
Hackle:	Brown and grizzly mixed
Cheek:	Jungle cock (optional)

Although the above is the standard pattern for this popular fly, it is the multitude of proven variations that make it so popular here in the Northeast. For example, the wing tied with two wood duck feathers seems to be far more attractive to trout than the teal feathers. And, tying red hackle fibers under the wing presents a variation that attracts fish as well as the original yellow hackle dressing.

Color is all-important and no other fly displays color more than the Hornberg. Tied with a green- or yellow-dyed teal the Hornberg will produce results that will amaze even the most critical of skeptics. Brown wings and white wings have also produced good results. It is obvious that the Hornberg, much like the Ghost series of streamers, has that basic appeal that allows almost all variations of the patterns to meet with success.

Don't be afraid to tie a Hornberg differently from the pattern inscribed in the indelible pages of some august book on fly tying. The Hornberg tied in sizes as small as a number 16 short shank hook, to a number 2 streamer hook will take some fish somewhere. I suggest tying them no smaller than number 14 short shanked, and no larger than number 8 on a 3x1 hook.

Do, however, vary the colors. Don't be shy about it and don't hesitate to experiment. The Hornberg is one fine fishing fly and it will serve you no matter what its dressing. In fact, the latest trend is to tie this fly in blue. And, wings aside, don't forget that the body does not have to be silver because gold tinsel works equally well. For added flash, you may even use embossed tinsels.

Even the hackle is not sacred. This can be varied as well as any other part of the fly. If you are prone to yellow for example, then by all means tie yellow hackle with the grizzly. A caveat is in order here.

No matter how you vary the fly, always include some grizzly in the hackle tied in at the head.

Trolling with lures for trout has never been a favorite method of mine. But in all honesty, there have been times when using a Mooselook wobbler has saved me the disappointment of going fishless. My favorites are the small ¼ ounce fluorescent red wobblers. Along with these I also carry an assortment of silver, gold, brass, white and red, and orange and red. Other trolling lures that have proved productive at times are the Al's Goldfish and the Flatfish in the smaller sizes, especially white and red spotted or all black.

When I use the Mooselooks, I employ lead-core line. For the Flatfish and Goldfish, I use monofilament line. There is usually no need to go deep with these lures because they primarily take fish only at the beginning of the open water season when the fish are plentiful and willing. But these lures will in no way replace the small streamer fly as top baits to drag through the water behind a boat.

One trolling lure for trout that has become a favorite of mine over the past decade above all the others is the Super Duper. When at times the trout stop taking a trolled fly sometimes even during the same outing, I go to the Super Duper.

Both gold and nickel Super Dupers will take fish. However, my favorite is the nickel Super Duper with the red head in sizes 502 and 503. The 502 is one and one-quarter inches long and the 503 is one and one-half inches long. Either size will work equally well, but I always start with the 503 size.

I use the Super Duper with lead-core line much the same as I would when trolling a fly. The exception being that most often it is not necessary to impart movement to the lure. There are times however, when sweeping the rod will make the Super Duper more attractive and during these sweeps trout generally hit the lure while it is settling downwards.

When using a Super Duper, I recommend employing a small snap swivel. My preference is a brass hued swivel in size ten or twelve. Super Dupers can twist a leader quickly. The swivel also makes the lures action more attractive to trout.

3

Modern Trout Baits

Today's fisherman does not usually dig in the garden for earthworms. Nor does he crawl on hands and knees on a rain-soaked lawn in search of nightcrawlers.

Salmon eggs, whole-kernel corn, bits of cheddar cheese, miniature marshmallows and Power Bait have eased the plight of the worm. Most modern bait fishing is done with that I call grocery baits, since all but the salmon eggs and Power Bait can he found in any supermarket. In fact, those who first suggested using these baits should be elected to the Fishing Hall of Fame. How much easier it is to find a supermarket than to find a bait dealer when in search of trout. And, how much cheaper the grocery baits are.

Although some anglers may be bothered by the idea of bait fishing for trout, the truth is that more people fish with bait than with flies. And, although fly-fishing is still the ultimate way to catch trout, many anglers who now look down on bait fishing began their quest for trout with a worm-baited hook.

It is definitely worthwhile to know how to catch trout with a spinning rod and a baited hook. This is often the only way a trout will respond to an angler's offerings. It is disheartening to watch a fisherman walk away with an empty stringer when the fish were willing and other fishermen around him were catching them. As simple as bait fishing can be, some anglers do not know the basics.

Becoming a skilled bait fisherman does not require a great deal of effort. It does however require some thinking on the angler's part. And it does mean carrying along all the store-bought baits on fishing trips.

Store-bought baits are relatively inexpensive, and if handled correctly, easy to pack in your fishing jacket or tackle box. You will have no excuse for walking away empty handed after a day's fishing, wishing that the can of corn had not been left in the cupboard.

Because Corn is the most popular bait, I'll begin with this little gem that is often referred to as "the golden nugget".

CORN

Many brands of whole-kernel corn are available on the market and if they are good enough for man then they are certainly good enough for trout. The less expensive brands are generally made up of kernels of different sizes.

A variety of baits are necessary if you are going to catch trout. Marshmallows, corn, and salmon eggs are a must. A jar of salmon egg juice will enhance the corn kernels.

These will catch fish, but it is best to buy a big name brand. Most of the kernels in the better brands are uniform in size and well suited for placement on a hook. Besides, the difference in price among various brands is not enough to warrant any concern over the budget.

If you are going to fish alone, your best bet is to buy small cans of corn. If fishing is a family affair, buy the large cans. I mix my purchases so that I can use whatever size is appropriate at a particular time. A plastic jar, preferably with a screw-on cap, will help keep your corn fresher longer. If you want, you may bring the unused corn home after each trip and refrigerate it. Soured corn does not deter fish; it actually seems to attract them. Trout do indeed use their sense of smell when feeding on the bottom and there is no accounting for taste.

Baby food jars and empty salmon egg jars also make fine containers for corn. The larger jars fit easily in a tackle box, while the salmon egg jars fit neatly into the pocket of a fishing vest.

An important part of a fisherman's tackle when using corn as bait is a can opener. I bring along a camping version of the old G.I. can opener. This small tool can be carried easily on a fishing vest simply by attaching it to the vest with a chain snap. However, Del Monte now makes canned corn with pull-tabs to open the can. Thus, cans of corn with pull tops now make the use of a can opener almost obsolete. But don't fail to bring an opener anyway since most brands do not yet provide pull off tops.

Gold hooks, where legal, should be used when fishing with corn. Over the years, I have become partial to gold hooks when bait fishing for trout. They are not only strong, with extremely sharp points, but they apparently do not deter the fish. If anything, they attract them.

Number eight or ten hooks are best for most trout fishing. These sizes are large enough to set into the jaw of large fish, yet small enough to be taken in easily by fish less than ten inches in length. The bait-holder hooks, those with slices in the shank to hold bait are best. For a marshmallow, corn, and salmon egg combination, I use size eight hooks. For corn or salmon eggs alone I use size ten hooks.

Hooks should be tied directly to the line. No swivels or snelled hooks should be used when bait fishing for trout. The lightest line test that you can safely handle should be used.

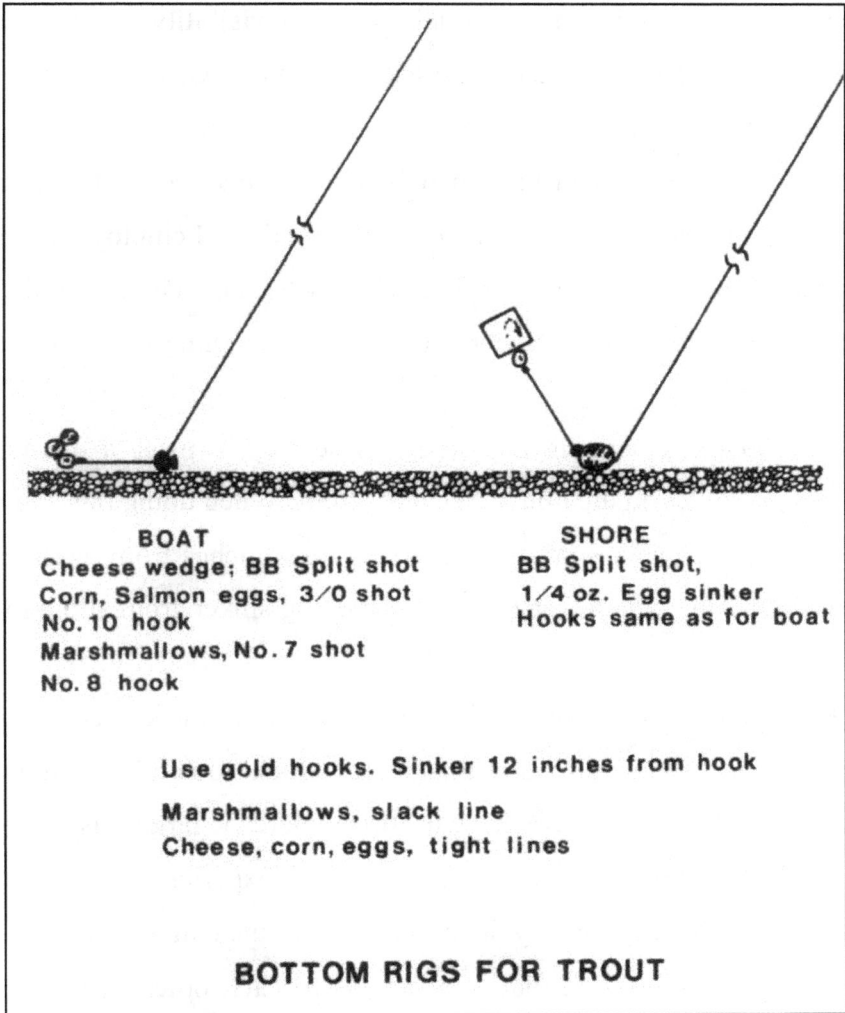

BOAT
Cheese wedge; BB Split shot
Corn, Salmon eggs, 3/0 shot
No. 10 hook
Marshmallows, No. 7 shot
No. 8 hook

SHORE
BB Split shot,
1/4 oz. Egg sinker
Hooks same as for boat

Use gold hooks. Sinker 12 inches from hook

Marshmallows, slack line

Cheese, corn, eggs, tight lines

BOTTOM RIGS FOR TROUT

For most trout fishing, four-pound test line is fine. In ponds with extremely dirty bottoms, six-pound test may be used to allow you to pull your hook free from snags.

My favorite line is Berkley Trilene XL green. It is small in diameter and much stronger than its stated breaking strength. However, it does require ones undivided attention due to its low visibility. If you have difficulty being a line watcher the use of Berkley XL high visibility line is best.

Weight is important in bottom fishing with small baits. I use the lightest split shot that will do the job. On calm days, I employ one BB sized split shot. On windy days, I use a 3/0 split-shot. There is seldom if ever a need to go to a heavier split-shot when fishing with corn for trout.

Shore-bound fishermen may find it necessary to place a quarter-ounce egg sinker on the line to reach the trout. When doing this, place a small BB size split shot one foot to eighteen inches from the hook after sliding the egg sinker on to stop the egg sinker from sliding to the hook.

Corn should be set on the hook so that the meat of the kernel only is impaled on the hook. No more than three kernels should be used. Do not assume that more kernels will attract more or larger fish. And although one or two kernels will take fish, my experience over many years has proven beyond any doubt that three is the magic number.

The kernels should be placed at angles to each other so that the cores are not aligned. This gives the corn a tantalizing action during its descent. It would be foolish to suggest of course that corn looks like natural food under the water. My experimentation over the years with corn as bait has proven the kernels work best when not aligned on a hook.

To use corn effectively often requires more skill than most anglers would expect. It is true that a trout will at times take corn with such abandon that the rod dips sharply and the fisherman need only set the hook lightly to begin retrieving the fish. On many days however, being a line watcher is of the utmost importance. This holds true with all baits, of course, but for some reason trout have a way of escaping all too easily with a kernel of corn.

On windy days or on days when the fish are taking the bait lightly, there should be little or no loose line to flap in the breeze. The line should be kept snug, the bail of the reel closed (always), and a sharp eye kept, not on the rod tip, but on the line. When the slightest movement is detected, the hook should be set sharply. You may become a bit trigger happy, but you will catch fish.

All too often I have seen anglers sit for hours without ever moving their bait. They are most likely products of the old school, which preached that a good bait fisherman must have patience in order to catch fish. There may be some truth to this adage when it comes to bait fishing. But the fisherman who moves his bait on occasion will take more trout. I never leave my bait down for long periods. I move it at least every five minutes. After a half-hour I retrieve it, and cast again. After all, the bait may be caught under submerged debris or among weeds on the pond's bottom. Or else a trout may be idly finning nearby, not recognizing the bait as being edible.

Fish respond to movement. When I move the corn, I always bring the rod up sharply. This makes the corn skip off the bottom before settling once again. Many of the trout I have taken with corn have struck after the bait had been moved.

Where it is legal, chumming should precede the use of corn. Simply broadcast a handful of corn out from the boat and cast into it. I usually chum before I begin to ready my tackle to start fishing. Do not empty the can of corn all at once. It is best to use as little chum as possible. Corn settling down to the bottom will attract fish. It is best to throw a handful of corn every ten minutes rather than all at once.

I use a slingshot purchased from an English tackle company to broadcast chum when fishing from shore. That way I can send the chum out further to where I choose to cast my bait. The slingshot has a small basket to hold about two tablespoons of corn. This was designed originally to chum when carp fishing. It works excellent for chumming any kind of fish.

SALMON EGGS

One of the all-time favorite trout baits, especially for rainbow trout, is the salmon egg. Although these eggs now come in several colors, from yellow to red, the best eggs are natural ones preserved and dyed deep red.

The problem with salmon eggs is that they are expensive. A jar containing less than one ounce often sells for up to $5.00. I suggest that you stock up during the preseason when these baits can often be purchased at a steep discount.

Because a small jar of eggs is so expensive, too many anglers fail to use salmon eggs correctly. They do not chum with these baits simply because of their dollar value. To use salmon eggs properly, a fisherman must chum with them. I can remember time and again, catching fish while other anglers nearby went fishless even though we were all using salmon eggs. The difference was that I chummed beneath my boat. To take advantage of eggs already used, I gut my trout as soon as I catch them.

Inside, there are usually salmon eggs that the trout have picked off the bottom. I then throw the once-used eggs back into the water and ice the fish.

Going fishing almost always incurs some expense, especially when you go out of state or travel a great distance in search of trout. A few extra dollars to assure success is money well spent.

When salmon-egg fishing, a gold hook is best. A number 10 hook is the ideal size. I stay away from the short shank "salmon egg" hooks for using salmon eggs. A regular shank hook is best to use because I use multiple eggs.

Once again, the magic number three applies to the bait. I impale three eggs on the hook, making sure to cover the barb of the hook. There is no logical explanation for why it is so important to cover the point of the hook in bait fishing. Certainly we catch trout on flies and lures where the hook is bare to the world. Over the years I have found that there is a marked difference when using bait with an exposed hook point. Fish generally tend to ignore the bait.

Although the magic number is three, there are times when a number 12 gold hook and single salmon egg will take trout. I can recall many times fishing for rainbows when one salmon egg worked better than anything else. Employing line as light as one-pound test in order to induce the trout to take the bait worked best in those particular situations. These instances are few and far between, so the basic three-eggs-on-a hook principle should be adhered to in order to assure fish on almost every outing.

Line test should be no higher than six-pound test, with four-pound test being the most suitable for general fishing. At times, line as light as two-pound test will be necessary, especially in clear ponds where the visibility is high. My Jonah Rod, an eight foot rod made with a fly rod blank virtually assures that I can catch large trout with bait and not worry about losing fish, even when using line as light as two pounds.

Trout can strip salmon eggs off a hook slicker than any con man ever born. There are several reasons for this. After salmon eggs have been immersed in water for a short period, they become soft. It is little wonder then that trout can suck the egg off a hook without telegraphing their presence to a fisherman. Furthermore, trout can remove the juices from the egg without removing the shell of the egg. How they do this is uncertain; but it happens often enough that one would suspect they are sometimes interested only in the contents of the egg and not the entire egg.

Fortunately, when used correctly, salmon eggs often bring a more favorable response from trout. The rod bends sharply under their weight as they pick up the bait and move off. Trout respond to salmon eggs more vigorously than to most other artificial baits.

Using salmon eggs requires some degree of savvy. The bail arm of the reel should be closed, and there should be no slack line at all. The rod tip will dip sharply when the fish has picked up the bait, providing you with a signal. There should be no loose line between you and the fish when setting the hook.

Here again, however, the bait fisherman must exercise his judgment. There are times when some loose line is necessary to allow the trout to swim away just far enough to take the bait fully without hindrance.

In using salmon eggs, a fisherman truly learns the art of line watching. These tender baits can be removed so easily that the slightest signal requires a response.

Salmon eggs are fragile and require some degree of care. Many freshly purchased eggs are too soft to use as bait. To harden the eggs so that they will stay on the hook, open the jar, place it upside down on a paper towel, and allow the juices to drain. After an hour, close the jar tightly.

To assure that the eggs remain in a vacuum, place a lit paper match into the jar and apply the lid. The brief moment it takes for the flame to extinguish is enough to consume the air trapped in the jar.

Salmon eggs that have hardened to the point where they cannot be applied to a hook can still be used as chum. There is no need to waste any of these valuable little gems.

CHEESE

A very effective bait, but one that is not very popular is cheddar cheese. It is a good bait for the fisherman since he can eat it while waiting for a fish to bite.

A block of cheddar cheese can go a long way when trout fishing. Chopped up, it is used for chum. And cut into small pyramid shapes and impaled on a hook, it will bring amazing results. Why trout like cheese is anyone's guess. But I have caught trout that were chock full of this delicacy.

Fishing with cheese is more difficult than with other artificial baits. Cheese, much like salmon eggs, does not stay on the hook for long periods of time. It is water-soluble and softens after a short while, and so it should be changed every time the line is retrieved.

Very often trout hit cheese while it is descending toward bottom. When this happens the line moves off sharply, so it is important to be alert to the possibility of this kind of strike.

With cheese, the best line to use is the lightest one you can fish comfortably with. Two-pound test monofilament is best but four-pound test will do. And, whenever possible, use no weight. If you must, a BB size split shot will more than suffice.

Be suspicious of any line movement. It may well be the wind that causes the line to stir, or it may be movement within the boat. But one thing is certain. Empty hooks will return to the rod tip of anglers who expect a rod-bending strike with cheese baits. Trout do not usually hit sharply on cheese, they instead become dainty critters, in most instances.

Once the cheese has been cast into the area of the chum, and if it makes it to the bottom, close the bail arm of the reel and remove any slack line. It is important to strike the fish at the very slightest sign that it has taken the bait. Cheese is easily removed from the hook and often there is only a slight indication of a trout's presence.

I have found that holding the line between my forefinger and thumb is the best way to quickly feel a trout's presence when fishing with cheese. It is tedious to be sure, but it prevents missed strikes.

During the cooler months cheese will stay relatively fresh without any special care. However, as the weather gets warmer it is best to keep the cheese iced until you are ready to use it. Not only will this bait deteriorate in water; it will also spoil in the heat. Soft cheese is already on the way to becoming useless as bait. If some of the cheese does soften cut it up and use it for chum.

MARSHMALLOWS

You don't need to toast 'em or roast 'em. All you need to do is keep them dry until you are ready to use them. And if they become stale, well, they are still appealing to trout. When used properly, they are deadly trout bait.

You cannot chum with small party-style marshmallows because these tasty tidbits float. But, to chum with something that resembles these little white sugary blocks, use large-curd cottage cheese.

Cottage cheese is a messy chum but it works. In all honesty though, it is not necessary to chum with a look-alike when using marshmallows. I use corn as chum almost exclusively now when using marshmallows or any other artificial baits.

A number 8 gold hook is best suited to fishing with marshmallows. I usually impale a marshmallow, a kernel of corn and a salmon egg on the hook. I call this my marshmallow salad. It is deadly for taking all species of trout.

Because marshmallows tend to float, they require a bit of weight to take them down. I use only enough weight to bring the marshmallow to the bottom and no more. This usually means a number seven split shot.

What makes the marshmallow so appealing to trout is probably more a matter of sighting. Because they are buoyant, marshmallows float off the bottom, making them highly visible to trout. When trout see this bait they usually take it in with gusto. In most instances, the fish has hooked itself by the time the angler is aware that he has had a bite.

There are some important factors to keep in mind when fishing with marshmallows. You can safely use six-pound test line and not spook the fish. The number seven split shot should be attached twelve to eighteen inches from the hook. A marshmallow will last approximately thirty minutes before dissolving in water. It is important to change the marshmallow, salmon egg and corn each time the line is retrieved.

The bail arm of the reel should be closed, but there should be some slack line. This loose line will allow the trout to inhale the bait and swim away. When it reaches the end of the slack line, it will hook itself. Most trout taken on marshmallows are deeply hooked, proving that the best way to fish this bait is to do nothing.

I use a small plastic food container to keep my marshmallows dry and fresh. At times I have added grated cheese to the container, but over the years I cannot say that it has helped. A plain marshmallow seems to work best.

There are now marshmallows on the market that are flavored, colored, and packaged fancily in little containers at high prices. The plain baking marshmallows found in markets are still the best. There is no need to get fancy when using this grocery bait. If marshmallows appear to be too soft to stay on the hook well, you can harden them a bit by leaving some out in the air. This will make them stay on the hook better. Fresh, soft marshmallows dissolve in water too fast and can be sucked off the hook too easily as well.

POWER BAIT

Since my first book was written, a very special man-made trout bait has come on the market. One that has made even novice fishermen catch trout as though they were experts. This medium is so popular today that store shelves empty quickly every spring. I am of course referring to Power Bait, manufactured by the Berkley Company. It is a putty like substance that adheres to a hook, has varying odors, and floats.

There are many colors of Power Bait and each seems to have a peculiar odor to attract trout. But the odd thing about Power Bait is that each fisherman seems to have a favorite color to use. And they all catch fish to some degree.

My over-all favorite color is rainbow. This is simply a mixture of green, yellow and orange. I have used all of the colors that have been marketed and I have concluded that rainbow is best. That is why my tackle bag is chock full of them. Orange and chartreuse are my second and third choices.

Using Power Bait is easy. It is clean and it lasts more than a year as long as the jar is kept tightly shut. I store my jars upside down but I am not sure that this truly saves it from spoiling, the tight lid is most important because air hardens the bait.

When using Power Bait assure that no water gets into the jar and keep the jar sealed between use. Power Bait is water-soluble and in time it will deteriorate in water. That is one reason to use dry hands when applying Power Bait to a hook. A hand towel should be used to keep your hands dry before applying Power Bait.

Treble hooks need not be used to fish with Power Bait. In fact, in some jurisdictions, treble hooks are illegal to use with bait. I use short shank, gold, salmon egg hooks when fishing with Power Bait. These hooks have a sliced shank to hold the bait.

A size eight salmon egg hook is best for using Power Bait. Simply cover the entire hook including the eye of the hook to the line with an amount approximately the size of your index fingernail.

Many fishermen keep their line taut while using Power Bait. While this may work fine during periods when fish are freshly stocked, or if you choose to try to lip hook fish so you can release them; the best bet is to use the slack line method.

With slack line the fish will swim off with the bait and take it in deeply, assuring that you will have it hooked well. However in this case releasing fish means cutting the line at the fish's mouth. If you choose to do this, do not lift the fish because you may cause damage to its internal organs.

Whether from shore or a boat the tight line versus slack line issue is moot. You can use both from either venue. The big difference is that from a boat you should use either a 3/0 or number seven split shot sinker and from shore a one-quarter ounce egg sinker should be used.

The egg sinker should be placed eighteen inches from the hook with a barrel swivel between hook and sinker to prevent the sinker from sliding down. The swivel also will prevent line twist.

WORMS AND NIGHTCRAWLERS

With the advent of grocery baits, the worm and nightcrawler have become second favorites of pond fishermen. These critters are still the staple of bait dealers and a great many fishermen buy them each year. But the truth is that the purchasers of these wriggly baits simply have not tried the artificial baits often enough to learn how successful they can be.

Worms and nightcrawlers as bait for trout in lakes and ponds leave much to be desired. When fishing for trout in ponds, worms are just about useless. It is the nightcrawler that will take trout best in lakes and ponds. This meaty bait still attracts brook trout, browns, and rainbows. But beware, with the exception of the brook trout, rainbows and browns prefer the grocery baits.

Medium-sized nightcrawlers are best for trout. There is no need to use the outsized nightcrawler, since this may present a problem when smaller fish are present.

One of the methods I use when fishing with nightcrawlers is to use a fly rod. That's right, and it works. I cast the worm out (with great difficulty) and shake out enough line for the bait to descend to the bottom near the point where it entered the water. This does not have to be too far from the boat. I then take a few feet of line off the fly reel and let the line set on the bottom of the boat.

When a trout takes the bait, the line will slowly creep through the rod guides. Always be certain that there is nothing obstructing the line so that it will move freely. Once the fish has taken the loose line, set the hook.

When worm fishing, I never let the bait set on the bottom for a long period of time. Every twenty minutes or so, I move the bait. Remember that movement attracts trout.

When using a spinning rod while fishing with nightcrawlers, I fish with an open bail. This is essential, since the fish must have time to take in the bait. To prevent the loose line from peeling off the spool, I insert it into a woman's hairpin, which is taped to the fore handle of my spinning rod. This holds the line so that wind or movement within the boat does not cause it to hang loosely and get into harm's way. When a fish takes the bait, the line pulls free so that the fish does not feel any pressure.

There are a few commercial line holders on the market that will do the same job as the hairpin. The hairpin is cheaper though and can be purchased almost anywhere. Most commercial line holders sell for around five dollars. Inflating a worm with air is a good way to keep it off dirty bottoms. A small plastic bottle with a hollow needle is used for this trick. Called Lindy's Worm Blower, this device fills a nightcrawler with just enough of an air bubble to make it float. You must be careful, however, not to inflate the worm in an area where the hook will be inserted.

Raising the nightcrawler off the bottom not only serves to keep it from becoming hidden under debris; it also makes the critter more visible to trout. This high visibility is what makes worm inflating an effective way to fish.

Catching and keeping nightcrawlers has been the subject of countless pieces. I'll not bore you with this subject. Simply use the method of care and preservation that you feel best suits your needs; or let the bait dealer worry about it.

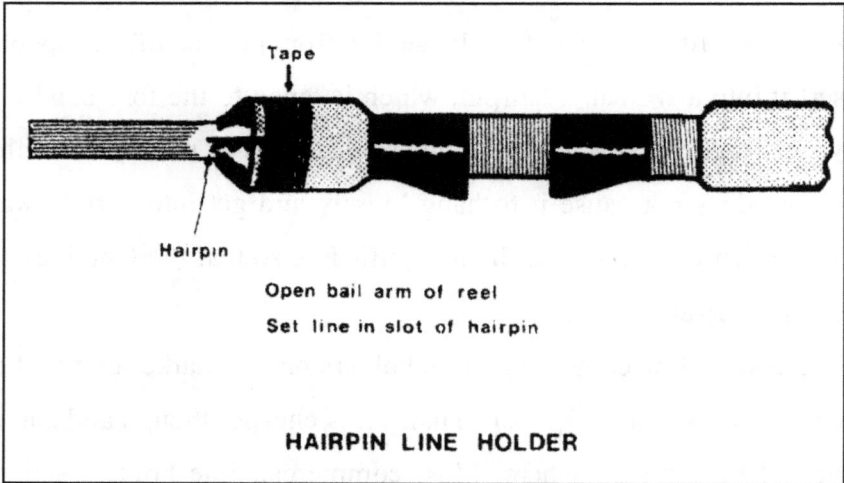

Tape

Hairpin

Open bail arm of reel
Set line in slot of hairpin

HAIRPIN LINE HOLDER

LIVE BAIT: SHINERS AND SMELT

I have used shiners and smelt for trout with great success, although I generally restrict my use of live bait to landlocked salmon and to those lakes and ponds where large trout can be found. Because they can work well however, we will discuss how to use shiners and smelt when flies and lures fail. Keep in mind that in some jurisdictions, in designated trout lakes, the use of live bait may be prohibited.

I first learned just how effective live bait could be at Lake Winnipesaukee and Great East Lake. These are large bodies of water that harbor landlocked salmon, lake trout, and brown trout. Although the lake trout have never responded strongly to my presentation of live bait during open water, the browns and salmon were, at times, extremely willing — especially when the water was windswept, creating a chop that salmon favor.

Drifting for salmon is not much different from drifting for brown trout. The technique is the same. For the sake of brevity, I will refer to shiners only in discussing live bait. Each time shiners are mentioned, keep in mind that if you are after landlocked salmon, smelt is your bait, and if you are after brown trout, then shiners are your bait.

Landlocked salmon and even brown trout will rise toward the surface in windy weather. It is during a blow that fishing with live bait is best. You can maintain a nice drift and hold the rod and line in your hand.

Hook the shiner through the lip on a number 8 hook. This will allow the fish to swim behind the drifting boat. To hook a shiner through the back under the spine would create an unnatural movement and would not attract even the most naive of fish. Tie the hook directly to the line. Do not use a swivel or snelled hook. A swivel may be applied five feet from the terminal end if you begin to experience line twist. Terminal hardware should be avoided whenever possible. Place a 3/0 split shot eighteen inches above the hook and you are rigged to catch both landlocked salmon and brown trout.

Pay out enough line to send the bait to about four to five feet below the surface. A half dozen sweeps of a seven-foot rod is about right. Keep in mind that when you are using live bait; you will be fishing from three feet under the surface during a chop to ten feet under when the water is calm. It will take practice to determine the proper depth for fishing shiners since all lakes and ponds are different in this respect. On the average, though, three to five feet will be most productive.

The best way to fish shiners is by drifting. When drifting, you must be prepared for a strike. You may hold the line in your hand, or you may affix it to a woman's hairpin. Simply tape the hairpin to the rod handle above the bail arm of the reel and insert the line into it. When a fish takes the bait, it will pull the line from the hairpin. It may be necessary at this time to take up the oars and hold the boat steady against the wind so that you are no longer drifting. Don't move toward the fish; simply hold the boat steady in the wind.

By holding the boat steady you will be able to tell if the fish is moving off with the bait, has stopped momentarily, or has dropped it altogether. Movement away from the direction of the strike because of drifting will make it impossible to tell if the fish is still on, since line will peel off the spool because of the boat's movement.

Another method of drifting live bait for landlocked salmon and trout is to attach a small float or bobber six feet from the terminal end of the line. You should attach a swivel to the line when fishing this way. Place the bobber directly above the swivel and attach six feet of line to the swivel. Use a barrel swivel for extra security. The bait may tend to cause a bit of line twist, which will be offset by the swivel. When a fish strikes, allow it plenty of time to take the bait. The small bobber will not cause it to become alarmed, so chances are you will be able to set the hook even after allowing it to run for the minimum twenty seconds it usually takes for the fish to take the bait down. A common cause of missed strikes while using live bait is an angler's inability to practice patience. Let the fish take the bait, don't be too anxious to set the hook quickly, and you will catch it.

The author catches his limit on opening day!

LURES

With the exception of freshly stocked trout, I have never found lures to be very good for trout. There are exceptions, of course. Some ponds and lakes will yield trout to lures regularly.

For the most part, lures are best for new fish that have yet to discover the delicacies of their new homes. Because we do catch fresh hatchery fish, perhaps a brief mention of some of my favorite lures should be a part of this chapter.

The way to work a lure for trout is any way that it will work. This basically means varying the retrieve, allowing it to sink, and being keenly aware of the slightest nudge.

Lures that I have found to be super for trout include the Al's Goldfish, in gold or silver; the Thomas Buoyant in one-sixth ounce size; the Fiord spoon and the Fiord Jr., both gold and silver; small Kastmasters; Flashfish; Mepp's Aglia size 10 and #1 plain spinners without hook dressings; Rooster Tails in white, yellow, or brown. The Panther Martin with a black and yellow dotted blade, as well as those with silver or gold blades is also fine. These should be the smaller spinners, and there is no real need to worry over body color.

I keep these lures in a small Plano pocket-pak and always have them on hand while fishing. Though I do not immediately use lures when fishing, I have caught enough trout with hardware to keep them handy.

The only advice I will offer is to keep those lures that are supposed to flash well polished and always hone the hooks to a fine point. There are some fine metal polishing products on the market to shine lures and spinner blades. For those who still smoke, cigarette ashes applied with a damp cloth will also burnish lures and spinner blades.

4

Bass Fishing

I have a special love for bass fishing. It is so natural, and because the fish are not delivered by truck to a pond or lake, our bass waters are not generally crowded by hordes of fishermen. I have fished for days on highly productive bass waters and never met another fisherman. This still occurs despite the fact that bass have become a highly popular fish since the advent of bass fishing organizations and tournament fishing.

Perhaps no other form of freshwater fishing has as many experts as the bass fishing fraternity. Everyone has their own pet lures or theories of fishing for bucketmouths. Pictures of bassmasters hefting stringers of heavy fish attest that they must be doing something right. In fact, of all the forms of freshwater fishing done in the Northeast, bass fishing has perhaps changed the most over the past decade. New lures, rods and reels, and bass boats have been developed at a record pace. The boats are usually equipped with large outboards and swiveled seats where fishermen can rest comfortably while controlling the boat with a foot pedal control and electric motor. All of these are now a part of the bass fishing scene. These boats require a boat trailer to haul and therefore require a good boat ramp to launch them.

Fishing in a bass boat is certainly much more comfortable than fishing from my small twelve-foot aluminum boat. The drawback of a bass boat, however, is that it prohibits us from fishing many of the excellent small ponds and lakes where only car top boats may he launched. So before we even begin to discuss my bass fishing tactics, which have proven to be very effective over five decades, let us discuss watercraft first.

If you own a large bass boat, that is fine. But you should also own a small semi-V hulled boat as well. This boat will enable you to fish the small bodies of water that are not able to accommodate larger vessels. Lunker hunters often overlook those little mud holes that harbor big bass. There are by far more small bodies of water ion the world than large. And because many are laden with restrictions concerning motor size, a small boat is a must. So whether you are in favor of large bass boats or not, it is imperative to own a small boat as well or you will miss out on some mighty fine bass fishing.

Roger Aziz enjoys some fine bass fishing in New Hampshire

I use a twelve-foot semi-V aluminum boat: the same boat that I use for trout or any other freshwater fish that I may pursue. It is not especially rigged for bass fishing. It is rigged for fishing, period. But more on how to rig a fishing boat later. Let's just say for now that a boat is a must for any pond or lake fishing in these parts.

THE BASS

A great deal has been written about bass. Their lifestyle, spawning ritual, preferred water temperatures, and the moon phases relative to fishing for them have all been described before. Let us here consider bass from the fisherman's perspective.

Bass are hearty fish that can live in small and often unclean bodies of water. They are survivors that can adapt to brackish water; cool, deep, clear lakes; and muddy, weed-choked ponds. That is why they are so plentiful.

Both large and smallmouth bass are exciting to catch. But there are marked differences between them. Some lures will attract both species, whereas some lures are better for one species than the other. In describing how to catch bass, I will discuss large and smallmouth bass separately. Keep in mind that much of what is said about largemouth bass can and will be applied to smallmouth bass. Certain fishing techniques thus need not be repeated when we discuss smallmouth bass.

LARGEMOUTH BASS

I have a few favorite bass lures that have served me well through four decades of bass fishing. I have used some for longer periods than others, but all have become a permanent part of my bag of tricks.

Anglers sometimes confuse themselves by carrying far too many different lures along with them. It is true that on occasion fishermen have caught big bass using lures that lay dormant in a tackle box for a decade. But the fact is that they might have caught more fish if they had used that wasted space filled by a seldom-used lure for another often-used favorite plug or lure in a different size or color.

Most of my bass are now caught with a small piece of plastic impaled on a large hook. If I were given one choice of lure to fish with, it would be a black plastic worm. I buy them by the hundreds and my tackle box offers mute testimony to my faith in them. It is chock full of the wriggly critters. If you are having trouble catching bass with a plastic worm, chances are you are becoming confused by the large number of rigs suggested by various bass pros. To further confuse fishermen, there is a multitude of different hook styles and weights to accommodate plastic worm rigs. This is fine for sporting goods sales, but for fishermen all these rigs can present problems.

I simplify my bass fishing with the plastic worm. I use a black, six-inch floater and a 4/0, high quality, black hook. This hook is large enough to imbed into the bony jaw of a bass and is also heavy enough to bring the buoyant worm down to the bottom in a slow tantalizing motion. I tie my line directly to the hook and impale the head of the worm so that the point of the hook is even with the head of the worm. It is that simple. I use no weights, and do not bury the hook point to make it weedless. This simple rig has captured countless numbers of bass for more than forty years.

To assure myself some advantage while bass fishing, I do carry other worms. I have purple and watermelon-colored worms, some with bright pink or orange tails, as well as black and purple worms with yellow spots. And although my favorite size is six inches, I bring some four and some eight-inch worms along. These are needed in case I feel that size or color may make a difference on a day when the bass are suffering from lockjaw. Because this so seldom happens, however, I suggest that you spend most of your time with the black, six-inch worm.

There are many soft baits on the market today, so many in fact that fishermen, especially new ones are often puzzled as to which ones are best. Tube baits and spider jigs can be very good especially in deep water because they are heavy and sink quickly. Once on the bottom a slow jigging motion will attract bass. I am not fond of fishing with rigs such as a spider jig and tube baits, but they can be very effective and should be part of every serious bass fisherman's tackle box.

Spinnerbaits are another of my favorite lures. My favorite is the Bush Hog because it is a well-made spinnerbait that holds up under heavy fishing pressure. It is wise to invest in well-made spinnerbaits because they are inexpensive enough. Cheaply made spinnerbaits often become useless after a bass has struck because the wire bends, distorting the lure's action.

In spinnerbaits, I prefer the one-quarter ounce, double-bladed, plastic skirted lures. These have accounted for more of my bass than any of the other weights, or the single-bladed baits. For color, my first choice is all white with white blades. I also use chartreuse, purple, yellow, and black. With black and purple spinnerbaits, silver or copper blades work best. With other hues I use spinner blades that match the body color.

I add a trailer hook to some of my spinnerbaits. This is usually a 3/0 hook with a large eye that can fit over the barb of the spinnerbait hook. I place a piece of plastic cut out of the lid of a coffee can onto the spinnerbait hook. I place the trailer hook facing down and opposite from the jig hook and then impale another piece of plastic on the spinnerbait hook. The purpose of the plastic tabs on each side of the eye of the trailer hook is to assure that the hook does not become disengaged while playing a bass. To make the plastic tabs, simply use a one-hole paper punch to cut them out of the plastic lid of a coffee can. One lid will supply enough little tabs to rig dozens of spinnerbaits.

Of all the minnow-type lures, I prefer floating Rapalas. Four-and three-eighths to six-inch models are the sizes that I have found best for largemouth bass. My favorite colors are silver with a black back or silver with a blue back. Gold with a black back has also been productive at times.

Floating Rapalas are my favorite because I can twitch them on the surface prior to retrieving them. Bass frequently strike the Rapala as it sits on the surface.

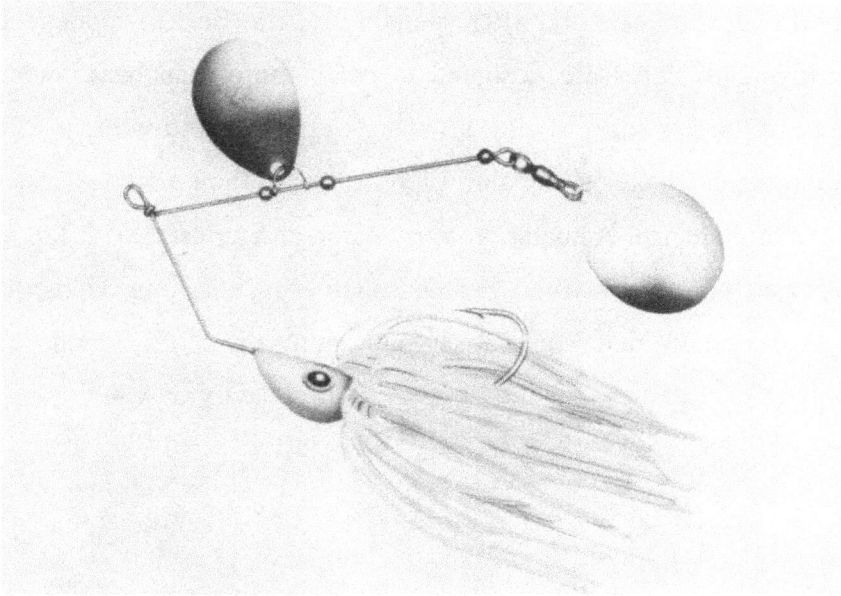

Typical double-bladed spinnerbait. Although unusual, these jig-type lures catch large numbers of bass.

I have a few favorite lures for surface fishing. I keep a good supply of Baby and Tiny Torpedoes on hand. I like the Jitterbug and the Hula Popper also. The space in a tackle box can be well utilized by discarding those colorful lures that you bought on impulse and carrying instead an assortment of these surface lures in different sizes and colors. And as part of your tackle you should have a few felt-tipped ink markers. I have often painted a Tiny Torpedo or Jitterbug all black or all green and turned poor fishing to good. This, despite all the talk of fish not truly seeing a surface lure's color.

With thousands of lures and plugs designed to catch bass available, it may seem odd for me to reduce my lure selection to so few. I have found over the years and after spending a great deal of money, that far too many lures are designed to catch more than bass. Indeed, many of the new deep diving lures are excellent. And with so-called fat plugs that shake, rattle, and roll, one would think that the bass do not have a chance. Actually, you can catch enough bass with the few lures that I have described to well satisfy your sporting needs. It is most important that you concentrate on using a few good lures properly, rather than wasting time weighing heavily on which plug to use next.

The noisy, erratic swimming motion of the Jitterbug has accounted for great catches of bass for decades. It is one of the top surface lures for bass.

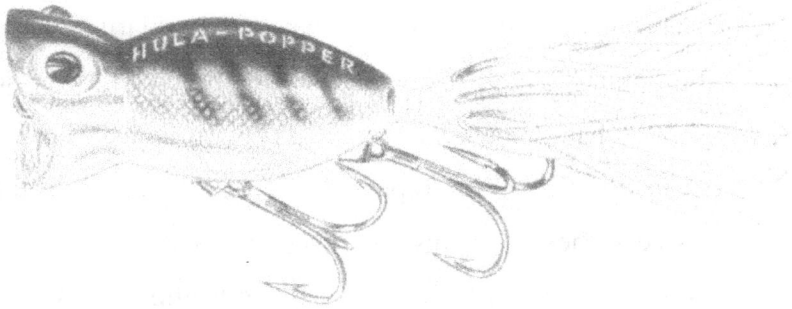

The Hula Popper is an all-time favorite of bass fishermen. Its loud popping sound brings bass to the surface with abandon.

SMALLMOUTH BASS

Black plastic worms and surface lures will take smallmouth bass as well as largemouth bass. I have found some lures especially good for smallmouth bass. Two of them, the Tiny Torpedo and the six inch black worm are used almost exclusively for my fishing for smallmouth now days. This is especially the case in smaller bodies of water of around 1,000 acres with many shallow areas.

In larger, deeper lakes I often fish with spinners because I can cover a great deal of shoreline quickly with these small lures. A yellow-bodied Shyster spinner with black dots is a very effective lure for smallmouth bass as is a Mepps lure. My choice of Mepps is the Black Fury in a one-third ounce size. This has a black blade with yellow dots and a yellow squirrel tail. The Comet 3 with a gold blade and squirrel tail in a one-fifth ounce size is also effective.

Although I seldom troll for bass, I have caught some fine smallmouth bass using a Flatfish or a Rapala. In the Flatfish, I prefer the two-and-one-quarter inch size, with the frog, perch, or silver-scale finish. I have also had some very fine fishing with orange and black dotted models of Flatfish. With Rapalas I find that the four-and-three-eighth inch size is best. Trolling however is more potluck fishing when applied to bass. When I seek bass I avoid trolling unless I have been fishless in a new body of water for more than two or three outings. If I catch a bass or two trolling, I then have an idea where to start. But for the most part, trolling is not the way to catch bass.

In using streamer flies for bass I prefer large deer-tail winged streamers. These are usually tied on number 2 extra long streamer hooks. These much resemble what today's striper fishermen call Deceiver Patterns. They are cumbersome to cast and tend to lie on the surface unless vigorously coaxed under the water, but they are attractive to bass. I use white or yellow-winged deer tail streamers. The body color is not important. I often tie as many with gold tinsel as with silver. The heads should be black and the addition of a painted eye is a plus.

Another streamer that I favor is a black marabou winged fly that resembles a leech. I have tied this for over thirty years and have taken countless smallmouth bass and numerous largemouth bass with it. This streamer is approximately four to five inches long and has a black chenille body and black marabou wings. The wing material is tied both at the rear and the front of the streamer. Once wet, it descends with a tantalizing wriggle and a slow pull and stop retrieve will entice the bass.

Smallmouth bass, more than largemouth, will take a streamer fly or deer hair popper readily. I often use streamers for bass in large lakes such as Wentworth or Winnipesaukee. In the spring, streamers will provide exciting fly rod action. Best of all, you can release fish without harm due to the fact that most will be lip hooked.

For both small and largemouth bass, fly rod poppers are exciting and many a bass fishing outing has turned into the highlight of my fishing day when these tough fighters have lunged headlong at a popper gurgling softly on the surface. What advice do I offer for these? Use any and all fly rod popping lures that suit your fancy. I have caught as many bass with cheap, twenty-five cent poppers as I have with the more expensive ones.

Of all the smallmouth baits, the crayfish has to reign supreme. Fished properly this live bait is irresistible to smallmouth bass, and most of the big smallmouth are taken with this critter.

TACKLE FOR BASS

Ask a dozen bass anglers how to catch bass and you will learn twelve different methods. Some of these might be grand schemes and perhaps costly, because bass have an aura about them that is mystifying to many anglers. They envision the fish as being more wary and more difficult to catch than most other species. The difficulty in catching bass may well be that there are probably fewer of them than, say, pickerel or perch. They can be stubborn to catch, but not necessarily. They can also be so easy to catch that they belie their reputation.

The first thing I would suggest when thinking about bass is to keep things in perspective. Fish simple. There is no need to become a gadget freak and purchase expensive tackle and lures. Large and smallmouth bass will take a plastic worm over any artificial lure that has ever been created. When I fish for bass I use two line test weights. In light cover I use eight-pound test line. In water that is extremely weedy, I use ten-pound test line. I also prefer to use Berkley Trilene XL line. I use XL high visibility line when using the plastic worm. This is a fluorescent clear blue line that affords me the extra visibility I need to watch my line while worm fishing. Its fluorescence has no adverse effect on fishing success. When using lures I prefer the Berkley Trilene XL green line. This is a super strong and low visibility line.

Before we go further, let me state that there is no such thing as an invisible line. A fluorescent line is indeed more visible under water than a clear blue line. However, I have never found the fluorescent line to be detrimental to bass fishing.

As far as tackle is concerned, there is no need to spend large amounts of money for so-called super bass-in tackle. How much finesse is needed to catch bass anyway? Forty-five years of fishing for bass suggest to me that tackle should be plain and simple.

I prefer spinning rods to bait-casting rods. I have both, but by and large I use the spinning rod more often and with more success. So much so, that I will not even discuss bait-casting outfits. If you have a penchant for bait-casting tackle, that is just fine. There is nothing wrong with it. But for most fishing, practical fishing, you don't need it. Remember that we are going to discuss bass fishing without complicating the sport. We are not discussing tournament fishing, or hawg hunting. Just plain old-fashioned bass fishing. This means catching bass whenever you go to the water for them.

I have tried many rods over the years and have usually used conventional seven-foot, medium-action spinning rods for bass, probably the most popular spinning rods among fishermen. Although these rods served me well, I always felt that they lacked something. Perhaps they did not have enough backbone when setting the hook. Although I caught myriads of bass with them and went along happy as a shiner in a bass tank, I had a gnawing feeling that somewhere out there was the perfect spinning rod for bass.

Rods for bass should have enough backbone to enable you to set a large hook, and flexible enough to allow you to place a lightweight lure, such as a plastic worm, wherever you wish. Short rods under six feet, and rods longer than seven feet may work, but less than ideally. Many of today's spinning rods have now been designed with bass fishing in mind, so you need not customize if you choose not too.

I use a medium-heavy seven-foot rod for plastic worm fishing. For casting spinner baits I use a six-foot, medium-heavy rod. For surface lures I use a medium-heavy, six-and-one-half foot rod. At times I use six-foot, one-piece medium-heavy to heavy action rods. In the heavy action rods I much prefer one-piece over two-piece rods.

There are so many spinning reels on the market that it is no wonder fishermen become confused when selecting a reel for bass fishing. To save time I am going to dismiss the closed-faced reel right off. I use conventional open-faced spinning reels only.

My favorite reels are no longer on the market. They are the Zebco Cardinal 4 reels. These reels have a rear drag adjust, conventional spool, and can carry 200 yards of eight-pound test and 150 yards of ten-pound test monofilament line. This is more than enough line capacity to fish for any bass. The reels have a very positive drag system that is unfailing. Unfortunately they are no longer available except occasionally at outdoors flea markets. For most bass fishing however, any good name brand conventional spinning reel will suffice. If you can find one that has a rear drag then by all means buy it.

I now also use skirted spool reels with long cast spools. The Daiwa SS 1300 and 1600 reels are two of my favorite skirted spool reels. They have an excellent drag system and are dependable. The SS 1600 holds 210 yards of ten-pound test line, while the 1300 holds approximately 180 yards of eight-pound test line. The drag adjustment is in front which is not where I prefer it to be. The reason is that I adjust my drag after a fish is on but more on that later.

Tackle boxes for bass fishing are becoming a problem. There are boxes to accommodate worms only, others for spinnerbaits, and still others simply designed for plugs. I use a tackle box that can do all of these things. It holds forty-five plugs, can easily store one hundred plastic worms and hooks in the well along with a dozen other items and will hold two-dozen spinnerbaits. It is not really as large as it sounds and I have used this same tackle box before the bass craze hit and all the new boxes were marketed. Tackle boxes are simply places to keep your lure selection out of harm's way. They should be sufficiently well organized for you to easily select a lure. The choice of tackle boxes today is as wide as all outdoors. But don't feel that you must carry several specialized tackle boxes along. The best lures will fit easily in a medium-sized conventional tackle box.

FLY FISHING TACKLE FOR BASS

Fly-fishing is becoming more popular than ever before. With more people fly-fishing and a new generation of fishermen beginning to recognize the bass species, it almost had to follow that the fly rod would meet the bass. Many of us however, have used fly rods for bass for years. I was fifteen years old when I caught my first bass on a deer-hair popper. I was fishing off the beach in October. Watching a bass dimple the surface, I cast the popper a few feet in front of it and the water exploded. The bass was hooked and so was I.

Fly-fishing for bass is not always the most effective method to catch lunkers, or for that matter, to catch a great many bass. You will catch enough bass to satisfy your sporting needs should you have a penchant for the long rod. I use the fly rod for bass when I tire of the spinning rod, which is usually during a good period of bass busting, or when I simply want to fish for the critters under ideal sporting circumstances.

Although I am not a fly rod purist, I have fished flies for over forty-five years and I have a great respect for the art. So perhaps we should discuss fly rod tackle for bass. In my region, during the spring season, smallmouth bass will take a deer-hair popper or a streamer fly with abandon. And largemouth bass will often provide some super action on warm summer evenings along the shoreline of small ponds.

The marriage of the bass and the fly rod has brought about a revolution in fly rod tackle. Rods are now available for bass fishing that did not exist twenty years ago. Fly rods, lines, reels, and new bass poppers are now marketed for bass fishing only. Is this new tackle necessary? Yes and no. This new tackle is fine and it may allow you to cast a fly more easily than could the older systems, but it is not necessary. You can catch bass successfully with the same medium-action fly rod that you use for trout.

I believe that a fisherman should have a rod to meet any fishing situation that he encounters. Just as the golfer would not use a wood on the green, a fisherman should not expect a fishing rod to do the impossible. The fisherman of course has a bit more control over his task. After the golfer makes his move, the ball leaves his club. Our fishing fly never leaves our control unless the line parts.

If you have a nine-foot graphite fly rod, you can assuredly cast a fly rod popper or streamer fly. First assure that the line weight rating for the rod is at least a seven or eight weight. The reels that you use for trout will work just fine for bass. These outfits will enable you to cast small poppers toward likely looking bass lairs. You don't need to make very long casts to reach bass. If you present the popper or streamer where you want it, that is fine. Unlike trout, bass will be attracted to the loud plop of a hair bug, popper, or streamer; they will not spook. But do not allow the line to create mayhem, splashing noisily on the water.

To send a fly to a bass does not necessarily mean that you must use one of the new fly lines that are designed specifically for fly rod bass fishing. If you can afford these lines, then by all means indulge in a spending spree and buy them.

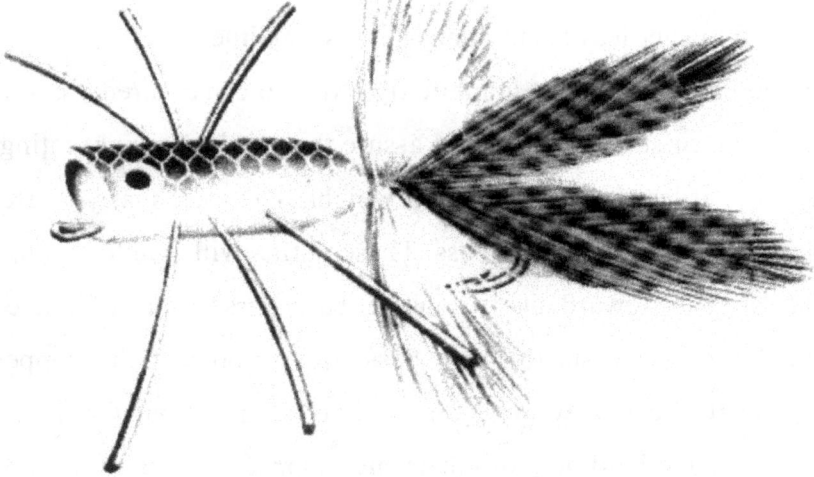

Fly rod poppers come in many shapes and sizes. Narrow-bodied poppers will make less noise and are best used on evenings when the water is calm.

I prefer the weight-forward fly lines for bass. I use these for most of my fly rod fishing simply because they enable me to cast better. While bass fishing, you will find as I have, that they will deliver a wind resistant streamer or popper much more effectively than level or tapered fly lines. If I had to select one style of fly line, it would be the weight-forward fly line.

Leaders for fly-fishing for bass need never be longer than eight feet. In fact, many times a shorter leader of six feet will suffice. The short leader will give you more control over the wind-resistant fly. Six- and eight-pound test leaders are best, and they do not have to be tapered leaders. A level piece of monofilament will serve you just as well as an expensive tapered leader.

The same fly rod tackle that you use for trout can be used very successfully for bass. You must however, choose your fly rod tackle wisely. A small, lightweight, seven-foot fly rod rated for a number four fly line will not provide you with the minimal power needed to cast a popper. When you use a fly rod for bass, the line should be at least a number seven weight, forward-weight line. If you want to set up especially for bass, think about number seven to eight weight fly lines.

Heavy-bodied poppers create more noise and disturbance on the water. These are best used when there is a ripple on the water.

BASS FISHING TACTICS

I have a special set of tactics for bass fishing. During the morning I begin fishing close to shore with a plastic worm. I cover all of the likely looking spots or good bass covers with which I am familiar. As the sun rises, most bass will move into deeper water unless they are in an area that provides shade, good cover, and a good supply of baitfish. In such a case they will likely stay close to shore. When cruising the shoreline during daylight, I look for shady areas where trees may cast a shadow. I also seek dark water areas. Bass are inherently drawn to areas where they feel protected or where they can wait in ambush for prey fish. Don't overlook dark patches of water or even muddy splotches. This is cover. After I try my hand at the shoreline, which is usually very productive, I move offshore. By now it is about 10 am. I then use either the plastic worm or a spinnerbait.

When using a plastic worm, I simply impale a black, floating, six-inch worm on a 4/0 hook. I tie my line directly to the hook, using an improved clinch knot or a Trilene knot. A Trilene knot is a clinch knot in which the line is wrapped around the eye of the hook twice before tying off the clinch knot. This knot, if tied properly, will not slip and is very strong. A tip when tying is to wet the knot with saliva or lake water before clinching it. This reduces the friction that results from drawing the monofilament line tight.

Cast the worm toward a likely looking spot in a high arc. Once the worm hits the water, close the bail arm. The idea is to leave some slack in the line. The worm will descend in a tantalizing manner, twisting and turning on its downward voyage. The point when the worm has touched bottom is the most important moment of worm fishing. Ninety percent of all strikes will happen on the first fall of the worm.

It is important to be a line watcher. If you keep an eye on your loose line, the bass will telegraph its presence. Bass do not usually take a plastic worm with smashing abandon. They suck it in and swim away with it. At times the line will be drawn out quickly and at other times it will twitch prior to being drawn taut as the bass moves away. Once the bass has taken the worm, point the rod in its direction, extend your arms forward, "giving it the rod," and when the line has been drawn tight, set the hook hard. After you set the hook, it is important to give the rod three more hard pulls to assure that the large hook penetrates the tough, bony mouth of the bass. And always fish the worm with the anti-reverse on. If you have a strike while busying yourself for some reason, this will enable you to still set the hook. If the worm is ignored on the first drop, wait a minute and retrieve slowly. Raise the rod tip upwards and reel in a foot or two of line. Next, lower the rod and allow the worm to settle. Once you have determined that the worm is near bottom, repeat the process. If a bass does not take the worm when it is near the boat, reel in quickly and cast again. There are times when a bass will take a worm close to the boat, but most often that is when a pickerel will strike.

Worm fishing is easy. The difficulty encountered by most fishermen is that they run out of patience. There will be weeds to clear from the hook and hang-ups on the bottom. It will be difficult to watch the line on windy days. And the worm must be fished slowly, which all too many fishermen do not enjoy doing. But if you give the plastic worm a chance, you will catch bass on almost every outing.

Spinnerbaits are so strange looking that I often wonder why a bass finds them so attractive. Perhaps it is the blade spinning slowly during the retrieve, or perhaps it is the color that attracts them to this bait. Knowing exactly why a bass will strike a spinnerbait is moot. What is important to know is that bass find them irresistible at times. And when they do, watch out. They smash spinnerbaits hard, often stopping your hand short during a retrieve.

At times I will use spinnerbaits when fishing close to shore, but I prefer using them when fishing offshore. I employ my deep-water tactic when I use these skirted, bladed jigs. I cast them as far as I can, close the bail arm, and allow the spinnerbait to sink. I use a countdown method. The depth of the lake determines how far to let the spinnerbait sink. I start deepwater fishing by allowing the spinnerbait to sink close to the bottom. On successive casts I fish it further off the bottom. Using the one thousand and one, one thousand and two countdown method works just fine.

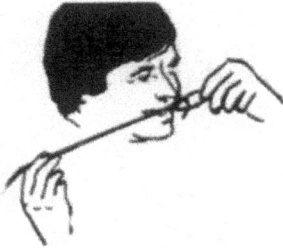

wet knot and draw down slowly

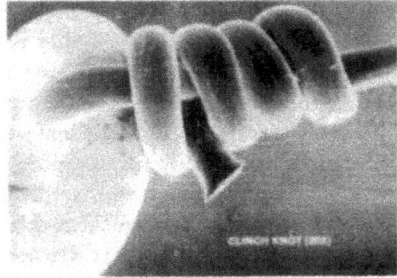

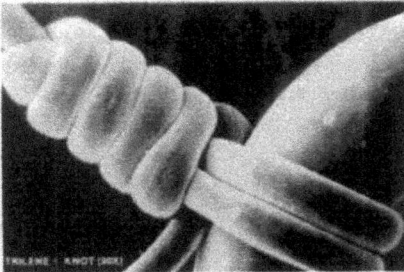

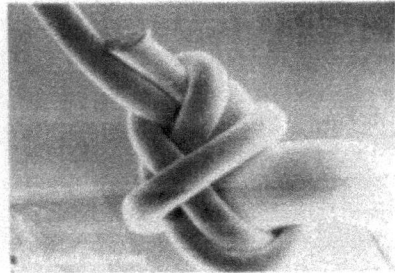

Both the clinch knot and the Berkley Trilene knot are good for securing hooks or lures. The Trilene knot is stronger because the line is looped around the hook eye twice.

It is not uncommon to begin to retrieve a spinnerbait and find that a bass has taken it on the fall. Be sure you are prepared when beginning the retrieve. Any resistance should be taken as a fish. Vary your retrieves, since bass may prefer a slow retrieve one day and a fast one the next. Vary the speed, use start and stop retrieves, and work the spinnerbait until you find the retrieve that the bass want. Spinnerbaits are simply fancy jigs and require angler-imparted action to work.

Weedless fishing is almost impossible to achieve. The closest I ever come to it is when I use a Dirty Bird to fish the salad-studded shoreline of a pond. Wherever the shoreline is thickly covered by lily pads there will be bass. The problem is presenting a lure to them without dragging half these water plants back to the boat after each cast. The Dirty Bird will accomplish this task. It is by far one of the most successful surface fishing lures for bass. It is also no longer manufactured so the few I own are priceless to me.

There are several weedless lures on the market today, any of which may prove to take bass. But fishing weeds is not easy no matter what lure you choose to use. I approach a weed bed slowly, easing near to the edge without actually abutting it. I cast close to shore and retrieve rather quickly so that the lure hops along the pads and makes enough noise to attract a fish below. Occasionally I will pause to give the bass time to follow up on the commotion. Usually on the next retrieve the bass will hit.

When I fish areas close to weed beds or just plain open water with a surface lure, I use the Baby or Tiny Torpedo. I use the Baby Torpedo, which is the larger lure, exclusively for largemouth bass. I use the Tiny Torpedo when fishing for smallmouth bass.

When I cast a surface lure such as the Tiny Torpedo, I close the bail arm as soon as the lure hits the water and immediately take in any slack line. I point the rod toward the lure and stay at the ready. All this is done while the anti-reverse is engaged on the reel. I let the lure set until all the ripples have vanished and then I twitch it once or twice and let it set again. I then begin to retrieve it two feet at a time, pausing briefly between retrieves.

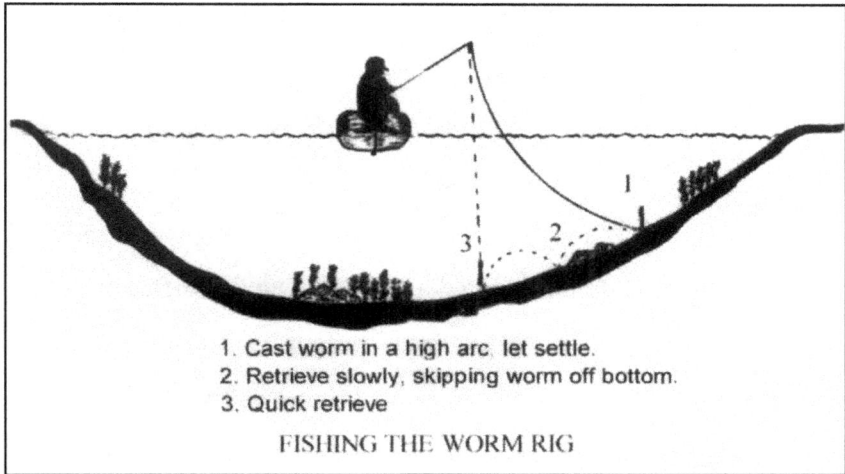

1. Cast worm in a high arc, let settle.
2. Retrieve slowly, skipping worm off bottom.
3. Quick retrieve

FISHING THE WORM RIG

Bass will most often take a surface lure shortly after it hits the water. But with action-type lures such as the Torpedo, they will also take it during the retrieve. It is important to be ready at all times and to strike the fish hard. After the first contact with the fish, set the hook deeply by giving it three more hard yanks with the rod. This will assure that the barb of the hook penetrates the fish. Too many bass have won their freedom from anglers who felt heavy pressure at the outset and failed to drive the hook home. When bass take to the air, they create slack in the line and that is when the lure is usually thrown. If your drag is set properly, you can set the hook hard without breaking your line. You can never set the hook hard enough when fishing for bass.

The Crazy Crawler and Jitterbug are fished much the same as the Torpedo lures. I have found it best, however, to retrieve these lures slowly and steadily. I only change my style of steady retrieve when the fish seem reluctant to strike the lures. These two lures have a built-in action that makes them gurgle as they swim toward the boat, and this results in some water-spraying explosions as the bass engulf them.

In surface fishing, the sight of a large fish breaking water to attack a lure is exciting. But some big bass opt to do it differently. They simply swim up to the lure and suck it in. Don't ever be fooled by this method of their taking a plug. Some of the biggest bass I have caught have taken the plug with nothing more than a dimpling of the surface. If you want to be a happy fisherman, be trigger-happy. Set the hook hard and don't become lulled into thinking that a small splash means a small fish. Not while fishing for bass with surface lures anyway.

Typical largemouth bass ponds will have a weedy shoreline with lily pads on the edge.

Surface lures are not only good during night fishing. They are good during the early morning hours as well. In the early spring some fine surface action can be had during the late morning hours. And during the summer, surface lures are very effective two hours before dark.

When using the Torpedo, the Jitterbug or the Crazy Crawler, avoid swivels. Tie the line directly to the eye of the lure. This imparts a much better action to them. You will also decrease losses by eliminating one more little device that can cause problems. Snap swivels do open at times and it is a rookie mistake if you lose a fish due to an unnecessarily complicated presentation. Simplify, simplify.

PLAYING BASS

After you have set the hook and set it well, there are a few things to keep in mind. The bass is a strong, energetic fighter and will seek to throw the lure free with violent head-shaking motions as it leaps into the air. It will also attempt to dive into heavy bottom vegetation to thwart you in your attempts to bring it to bay. This is where having a properly set drag and knowing how to handle a fishing rod is of the utmost importance.

Prior to fishing, set the drag so that it is just tight enough to slip prior to the line breaking. You don't need scales and expensive testing equipment to do this. Simply grab the line several feet away from the spool and pull until it feels tight but not too tight. If you have a partner, have him pull the line from beyond the rod tip while you hold the rod. The line should pull without breaking. If it appears too tight, loosen the drag.

There is an old rule that says that once a drag is set it should never be tampered with while playing a fish. That may be a good rule of thumb, but it doesn't always work out well for the fisherman. Drag is friction and friction caused by a fish running line through the mechanics of a drag system causes heat and friction thereby increases. So there will be times when the drag should be readjusted while playing a fish. You will develop a feel for those times as you go along. One suggestion I might offer is that you loosen the drag if necessary while playing a fish, but don't tighten once the battle has begun. This will allow a fish that is tired but not beat to take line, thus tiring it even more so that it comes easily to net. By loosening the drag, any surges by the boat will not result in a snapping of the line. After you have loosened the drag, if you need to apply more pressure for some reason you can do it with your index finger.

Monofilament fishing line has stretching ability. This is built into the line and is not an accident of manufacture. A certain amount of stretch is necessary to assure that the line won't snap every time pressure is exerted upon it. Too much stretch, however, is not good because it makes setting the hook difficult and sometimes impossible. When you have cast toward a likely looking spot and you have plenty of line out, it takes three times as much effort to set the hook as when a fish is close by. Once you have retrieved a great deal of line and you are playing the fish "short," there is greater danger that a sudden lunge by the bass will snap the line. That is why backing off on the drag is permissible.

When a bass takes to the air with a plastic worm imbedded in its jaw, drop the rod low and allow slack line between you and the fish. This will assure that the line doesn't snap or that the hook will not tear out of the flesh. When playing a fish with a heavier lure, such as a surface lure, raise the rod upon the leap. Keep the line tight and if you want to catch fish more than watch acrobatics, lean on a jumper. When a bass is turned in mid-air it becomes confused and the fight is taken from it. It will still battle, but it will be reluctant to take to the air again. Remember, leaping bass can win freedom easier than those that battle underwater.

When fishing in or around weeds, make sure that you lead the bass away from the vegetation. If it is seeking to dive deep into heavy weeds, try to stop its run and bring it to the surface. If you are fishing by a lily pad bed, try to bring the fish into open water. This can be done within the first few moments if you establish enough pressure and posture the rod away from the pads. One trick I often use is to position the rod so that the fish momentarily swims out from the cover of the pads. When it does this, I then start to play the fish toward the weeds by aiming the rod tip toward them while retrieving. Bass will generally swim away from the direction of the pressure, so this way it will not want to enter the weeds.

Once a bass is beaten and by the boat, it can be landed in one of two ways. With a plastic worm, you can place your thumb and forefinger in its mouth and bear down on the lower jaw. This will immobilize the fish and you can lift it over the gunnel. Or you can use a net. I strongly suggest using a fairly large net. There is no surer way to lose a bass than to beat on it with a net too small to do the job. Landing nets are relatively inexpensive and a sturdy, large net should be used.

5

Best Fishing Times

SEASONS

Let's discuss the best times to fish the various methods that I have presented in earlier chapters on catching trout.

For fly fishermen in the Northeast and elsewhere, March and April will mean catching freshly stocked fish. These new arrivals will take flies, baits, and lures, solely because they have not yet adjusted to their surroundings and the available natural food supply.

By May, after the fish have become acclimated to their surroundings and when hatches of various insects begin to appear, the trout will feed on more natural foods. They become selective and offer fly fishermen a bigger challenge. By July, trout head for deeper water and the comfort of the thermocline, that layer of water well beneath the surface where there is an ample supply of oxygen.

Most of your fly-fishing will consist of fishing with wet flies or nymphs. The wet fly by far will account for most of the trout taken by casting a fly. That is why I ignored the dry fly patterns in earlier chapters. For the few dyed-in-the-wool fly fishermen who scout the ponds diligently in search of rising trout, carrying an array of various flies, there is indeed some dry fly fishing to be had. It would be wiser in general though to concentrate on wet flies since they will account for most of the trout you will catch.

Wherever you live and fish, once the water warms, it is time to turn to lead-core line trolling. But before we go further, let me say that lead-core line fishing is good throughout all of the seasons. I turn to it later in the season because I prefer to catch trout on lighter tackle whenever possible. There is no other reason. Of all the fly-fishing methods, lead-core line fishing has been the most consistently successful for me during the period of open water.

June is the time I turn to lead-core line. By then most of the fish have spread out into the deeper areas and it may require some searching to find them. By trolling, you will be bringing the fly to the fish and not waiting for a chance meeting. You will also find the right depth and be able to concentrate in that productive zone. When casting a fly, the depths can be covered, but much too slowly, making it almost impossible to find trout during an average outing. Remember that we are talking about fishing that is intended to take "luck" out of the sport.

By mid-September trout fishing begins to pick up again for the fly fisherman in many locals. This is mainly because lots of jurisdictions stock their ponds and lakes with surplus fish, thus providing us with another new season. These fish will take flies readily, and fly-fishing can be sustained until the shank end of October and often into November, even in the Northeast. The weather plays an important role at this time; the fish do not necessarily remain cooperative once the water is thoroughly chilled to just below freezing. Not if you fish with small wet flies, anyway. At this time it is best to use small streamer flies that can be cast or drifted behind a boat. For those of you in the more temperate climate zones, your season is even longer.

Bait fishermen can look forward to good fishing in most states throughout the year. Whether the fish are newly stocked or have been resident for a while makes no difference. Trout adore baits and can be taken at almost any time with any of the baits described in Chapter 3. While Power bait is perhaps the most effective of the baits nowadays, no one bait is best for a particular time of year. They are all good where there is open water at any time of year. Do not hesitate to use bait and you will find that you no longer have to worry about seasons. In early spring, shore fishing will often yield results as good or better than boat fishing. As the water warms, the fish will tend to seek the spring holes or cooler areas of a pond or lake. This tendency works in favor of the bait fisherman because trout are usually congregated in a small area, or at least will frequent the "comfort" zone daily. Fish may leave this comfortable area in search of food if they become desperate, but they cannot stay out of an oxygenated and cool zone for very long. If you find the holes that harbor fish and present food to them, they will take it ravenously. That in essence is what makes bait fishing such a highly productive method. After locating a hotspot, you can present the bait time and again in the same area and catch fish day after day.

In summary, the best time to fish with flies in the Northeastern trout ponds is during the months of May and June and again during the latter part of September. The best time to use lead-core line is any time during the open water season that you want to find trout. And the best time to use bait is anytime at all.

TIME OF DAY

The time of day is just as important as the time of year when fishing for trout. In fact, the time of day is closely related to the seasons. New fish will feed at any time of day. Practical fishermen speak of new fish. Those who are deluding themselves pretend that we never come into contact with them. The truth is we catch them both wittingly and unwittingly on more occasions than we can count. When we speak of trout fishing in the Northeast, we are largely speaking of hatchery-raised fish and we must be willing to understand them.

So it is important to note that "new" fish will feed all day during their first few days, and sometimes for weeks in their new surroundings. They are constantly hungry since the dinner bell no longer rings on schedule. They are vulnerable and they strike savagely for long periods, while barely nibbling at other times. They will almost always feed whenever bait is presented to them, which makes fishing for new fish so appealing to many anglers. We have been weaned on hatchery trout and it is this fish that we have come to understand.

Before going further however, I would like to say that there is no shame in fishing for hatchery-reared fish. The truth is that after they have been in a lake or pond for any length of time, the survivors become wary and can present a challenge. Wild trout on the other hand are very easy to catch in most cases. Unless they are pursued often enough, they are just as vulnerable as a hatchery-reared trout and in many instances more so.

When you fish for trout with bait, keep in mind that your knowledge of the environment will help you determine the best time of day for fishing. If you are fishing a pond or lake that has been recently stocked, you may take fish throughout the day. If it has not been recently stocked but you are fishing during the cooler days of spring, you can again depend upon cooperation from the trout at any time of day. They will be continuously foraging. You may simply have to apply a bit more patience.

If you are fly fishing, the trout may rise in spurts, but flies fished well below the surface will take fish regularly during the day. That is what makes trolling with lead-core line so effective. You find the fish. They don't happen to come your way. When casting a fly during the cool months, any time of day is good. You should consider though, that if it is a bright day, the fish may be willing but they will be deeper, so you will have to fish the fly deeper and more slowly than you normally would.

As the weather warms and the pond or lake stratifies, it becomes apparent that the fish will become less inclined to leave their comfort zone. During July and August especially, the best time to fish is from daybreak until about 9 am. After that, the fish may cooperate, but they will be difficult to find and if you find them, they may be reluctant to feed. Having fed heavily during the early hours they may be content to hold in comfortable water and save their energy. Later on in the day, as evening approaches, they will begin a feeding binge once again.

Brook trout will feed until dark and stop. Browns will feed at night. Rainbows, bless their souls, will give you a thrill the last two hours of daylight on any summer evening. From about 7 p.m. until dark, you can count on some rainbow trout action at any of your favorite trout holes. But don't despair, the brook and brown trout will also oblige. They simply are not as predictable at dusk as is the rainbow.

When trolling with lead-core line, fly-fishing, or bait-fishing, keep in mind that the best fishing hours depend upon the seasons. There is no separation between the two. You can fish all day during the colder months and early and late in the day during the warmer periods. In the fall, don't start fishing until at least 8 am. on sunny days. The water warms slightly and the fish become more active. With this in mind, you will catch more trout in less time and not face the frustration of spending fruitless hours on a pond when you can be doing something else, like tying flies or wrapping a new rod. Unless you are looking for a healthy tan and don't mind sitting long hours waiting for a bite, plan your outings to take advantage of the best times to catch trout.

In some lakes, trout fishing is good all day long even through the summer months. In fact I often fish some of these excellent trout waters later in the day when the early-bird fishermen have left.

WEATHER

Weather indeed plays an important role in the quest for fish. No matter what the species, fish are affected by the moon, temperature, and barometric pressure. Because this book is not intended to be a science lesson, I will not go into detail about any of these. I will instead discuss my experiences with weather and fishing. My observations are gleaned from years of reading, doing, and sometimes, but not too often, thinking.

I used to go fishing whenever I could. Being a workingman, I did not always have the luxury of choosing my fishing times. I generally went even when my better judgment suggested that perhaps the fishing might not have been the best possible. In doing this time and again, I formed some opinions about weather apart from any scientific theories relative to weather and fishing. Now that I am retired and able to fish almost every day, my experience has proven that my opinions regarding fishing as related to weather were sound.

Fishing in the rain has never proved to be better or worse. In some cases a rainstorm that interrupted a dry spell has turned the fishing from fair to good. If the fishing was good to begin with however, rain did not make it any better. It made it more difficult to fish because of wet tackle and because of chilled bones when the weather was cool, or a sweat under a raincoat when the weather was warm. Rain has never been an ally of mine while fishing. Do trout bite better in the rain? My experience suggests that they do not.

Hot weather can adversely affect the fly fisherman. If he is a purist he may well think that soaring temperatures will produce poor fishing because the fish will be deep and usually offshore and actually this is true for his methods. Indeed trout will be deep, but the fishing can be and usually is good. Hot, steamy weather is excellent for fishing. If you are bait fishing the spring holes, this is exactly the type of weather you want. You will know for certain that the trout are congregated in the spring holes. You will catch them regularly. They are comfortable down below. They just cannot range too far for too long. Thus bait fishing for trout during hot weather is exceptionally good.

During hot weather the pond or lake stratifies and you can troll the thermocline with lead-core line. This area is rather narrow compared to the pond's overall depth and once you find the depth in which to fish you will consistently take trout. Hot, steamy weather is by no means the nemesis of anglers. It has served me well for many years and accounted for many stringers of trout taken both with bait on the bottom or with trolled flies.

Cool weather, such as that found in the spring and fall, is also good. It is even better if on a given day the temperature rises by a few degrees above that of the previous few days. This seems to turn the fish on. Let's remember that we are not considering moon phases here, or other such complex changes. We are dealing with what we can easily understand; the weather around us.

Cool weather can turn off fishing when it follows on the heels of a hot spell. I have always found a cold front to be detrimental to my fishing aspirations. When I feel a cold front coming I keep the rods hung on the rack and tie fishing flies or count salmon eggs.

Periods before and after a storm have also been good for me over the years. I look forward to these periods, but you must be cautious. Fishing when a storm is brewing can be dangerous. Always be keenly aware of lightning. No fish is worth risking your life for. After all, the fish will be just as willing right after the storm subsides, so don't take a chance.

If you insist on fishing during a storm, be sure to use a fiberglass fishing rod. Graphite rods are highly conductive and will attract lightning.

Changes in barometric pressure, up or down, have always improved fishing for me. Because you can observe these changes yourself, there is no need to run out and buy a barometer. Simply watch the weather, listen to the radio, and develop a feel for those weather patterns that provide the best fishing. After a while, you will know which days are most apt to provide good fishing. But take it from me; even if the weather is not super, go fishing anyway. It is on those days when most of the fish don't cooperate that the lunker usually does.

BASS: SEASONS, WEATHER, TIME

There is a distinction between trout and bass apart from their physical characteristics, biological needs, and feeding habits. The bass is not, as an angler once said, a universal fish. It is a unique fish. If you can catch bass, it does not follow that you can catch trout. Trout fishermen, on the other hand, cannot readily apply trout knowledge to bass. The large and smallmouth bass are in a class of their own. They require expertise, but not the finesse in approach that a rising trout would require. And bass respond differently to weather than do trout.

I have taken bass in "holes" and have had action reminiscent of fishing a spring hole for trout. But this was more because of my thinking than theirs. They certainly did not congregate in one spot because the water was cool and they could not leave it. They have a wider range within which they may move in their watery world.

Although bass can be taken through the ice, and I have caught many fine specimens this way, they respond better when the water is between sixty-five to seventy-five degrees. In the spring when the water reaches forty to forty-five degrees, they will start to become active. And most important, as the water temperature reaches sixty to sixty-five degrees, they begin to acquire the spawning urge. At this time they are so susceptible that many states have prohibited bass fishing altogether in the spring while others have special regulations during the spawning period.

Over the years I have found bass fishing best from May through June in the Northeast. I know it can be good in April and I have both caught and witnessed some fine stringers of large and smallmouth bass at that early time of open-water fishing, but I prefer late May through June to begin chasing the bucketmouths and bronzebacks. During these two months they are most active. Best of all, many of them have usually finished their spawning ritual, which incidentally, is a harrowing experience for the bass.

During the warm months, there can be no more pleasing form of fishing than casting a lure along the shoreline of a bass pond. No matter how hot the weather, I have found the bass will cooperate if I put in the time to fish for them. Summer fishing is not as good as spring fishing but certainly worth the effort. Toward fall, the bass begin to feed in anticipation of winter and again the fishing peaks. Bass are natural creatures and compete with their hatchery-stocked rivals for the hearts of anglers.

Although good bass fishermen can catch them at any time of the year, the best times are May and June, and again from mid-September through October. The earlier months yield heavy, egg-laden fish, and the later season yields hogs that are shoring up for winter. In between, we catch the hungry ones.

There is some uncertainty concerning the best time of day for bass fishing. In the spring and fall, I have had my best luck well after sunrise. About eight or nine in the morning has always been a productive period for me. During the summer I like to fish from dawn to about 10 a.m. and again from dusk till dark.

Bass can be and are taken during the day and certainly at night. I have restricted my fishing to the dawn and dusk hours because I like to see what is happening. The leap into the air, the struggle by the boat, the thrill of seeing it swim away when I release it. I do not enjoy fishing in the dark.

When it comes to weather and bass fishing I have always felt that weather is very important but in all honesty I don't know why. I have had some bonanza days when a cold rain poured on me. I have enjoyed some excellent catches on days when the wind swept a lake so fiercely that only my inability to keep watch on the line prevented me from catching dozens. And I have experienced some of my most exciting fishing during August, when the heat literally caused the sweat to pour from my brow.

The variety and length of my experience has led me to the following conclusions. I have done very well prior to a storm, but not just after a storm. This has not been true for trout, only for bass. I have done well in the rain. Perhaps this is because the raindrops covered my noisy approach or my presentation of a lure. I am still not certain. And I have done well on hot summer evenings. I will add at this point, though, that when the weather is extremely hot, it is best to fish late in the evening about two hours before dusk and at dawn until 9 am. Otherwise when it comes to bass fishing, I would suggest that you fish whenever you have the chance.

6

Tackle Tips

SETTING UP A BOAT

There is not much more that fishermen can do to enhance their chances of fishing success. Or for that matter, to make things a bit more comfortable. Fishing tackle and boat manufacturers have just about thought of everything, right? Wrong.

Let's assume that most of us do not own a bass boat, whether by choice or because of a lack of funds. We own instead, a small twelve-foot semi-V hulled boat or a Johnboat. This tin lizzy is the craft that is going to make us world-beaters when we fish our favorite trout or bass ponds. They are relatively simple. They have seats, a place to set oarlocks, and they don't leak. What more can be done to these simple boats?

The truth is, much can be done, and for very few dollars — for less than the price of a dinner for two or a ball game. And a small fishing boat can be modified in less than one afternoon of light labor to enhance our fishing. Let's discuss how we can make a small fishing boat a wee bit better.

For one thing, a car-top boat can present problems. Most of us do not resemble Charles Atlas. Eighty pounds of aluminum boat may prove to be too much to lift atop a car. There are ways to do it alone though. One way is to buy a one-man boat loader. These retail for about fifty dollars and can be purchased from several places, the most popular being from a marine catalog from one of the big mail order houses. The boat loader is simply a bar that attaches to the trailer hitch of a car (a bumper hitch will do) and is secured by a large bolt. At the top is a large double clamp that rotates on the bar. The stern of the boat is set into the clamp and secured by two screw-type fasteners. You then lift the bow of the boat, and move it toward the front of the car onto your car racks. It is that simple. The entire boat loader or the clamp only, can be removed and stored in the trunk when not in use.

Getting the boat to the car in the first place is a simple problem to solve. A large dolly wheel, available at most junkyards, can be purchased for fewer than five dollars. They are twenty dollars when purchased new from a hardware store. These can be secured to the bow plate of an aluminum boat by four nuts and bolts after measuring and drilling four holes so that the wheel is centered on the bow plate. The wheel should be at least six inches in diameter to roll easily over rough terrain.

With such a rig you will be able to bring your small boat almost anywhere that you can walk. If you are fishing alone, it is your partner. If you have youngsters it is their substitute until they are old enough to help. Most important, it means independence. You never have to fish from shore because a fishing partner whom you depended on to help with the boat failed to show on time, or at all.

In my boat I always place several small metal rope cleats to secure an anchor line. I place two on either side of the bow area and two in the stern area in the same manner. This allows me to tie my anchors off on either side of the boat.

I also place four large eye-bolts, two each, on each side of the boat fore and aft. These are used to secure fish stringers, bait buckets, or any other items I want to tie down or hang over the gunnels. The eye-bolts should not be placed too close to the cleats.

In the stern I place an aluminum bicycle basket on the right or starboard side. If I were left-handed, the basket would be placed to my left. This basket is used to store binoculars, cameras, and anything that I do not want to lay on the deck of the boat. It keeps the items high and dry. It can also be used to hang a few lures at the ready.

For towns where boat plates are issued to fish certain restricted waters, I have a way to remove and affix new plates easily. I measure the plate and drill holes completely through the stern. This does not harm the boat because the holes are made high above the water line. I then affix the plate with bolts and wing nuts. In this way, I can remove old plates and attach new ones within minutes without tools. Just be certain to tighten the wing nut by hand only. Also in the stern, I attach an eyebolt to secure a motor safety chain. None of these items will interfere with you while fishing. Indeed, they will enhance the boat and make fishing a bit easier and more comfortable.

On at least one seat of the boat, preferably the center seat, place one of those inexpensive bass rulers. Be sure to buy one that measures at least two feet long in one-inch increments. This handy ruler will allow quick measuring of fish. In many jurisdictions, there are size limit regulations that require us to be certain that we do not keep short fish.

Oars should not be ignored. There can be nothing more annoying than worrying about oars slipping into the water when you grab for a rod while trolling. I use pins to secure my oarlocks to the oars. Carefully measure the oar by sitting in the boat and setting the oars in the position that you will hold them while rowing. Mark them clearly and drill holes a bit larger than the pin. Drive the pins through the oars and oarlocks and flatten the pin ends so they won't slip out of the oarlocks. If you do this, you will never have to worry about losing an oar when you release them to grab your rod. An oarlock rarely drops out of its holder. Even if this occurred, the oarlock would not be lost since the oar will float and you can retrieve both the oar and the oarlock. A pair of oarlocks with pins retails for around ten dollars.

In fresh water I prefer mushroom anchors. I have never found much difference between the rubber-coated or plain metal anchors. Being quiet is the fisherman's concern. Coating an anchor simply will make a careless sound a slight bit less metallic. I use two ten-pound anchors and always place one fore and one aft while trout fishing. For bass, if alone, I simply drop one anchor over the bow. When fishing with a partner, I use both anchors.

A good three eighths-inch nylon rope should be used to hold the anchor. Cheap ropes tend to rot and may result in a lost anchor. I mark my anchor ropes every two feet with a black ink marker. This enables me to know roughly just how deep the water is where I am fishing. It is a cheap fish-finder, but most important, it enables me to know if I am indeed over a favorite fishing hole. On the free end of the rope, I tie a knot so that the anchor rope will not slip through my hands if ever I fish in water deep enough to reach the rope's end. Always have at least fifty feet of anchor rope per anchor. This is plenty for most of our lakes and ponds. And remember, when you are anchored in the wind, or on a large lake with only one anchor, always let out three times the amount of line as the water is deep. This will enable you to ride any swells created by waves or the wake of large boats.

When fishing from a boat, a large, long-handled landing net is of extreme importance. Not only will such a net assure that you can safely land a fish, but most important, there will be no need to lean over the gunnel, thereby endangering yourself and others. When alone a large net of this type is as good as a partner.

If you fish at night, the law requires running lights. If night fishing is not in your plans but there is a chance that you may occasionally find yourself coming ashore at the brink of darkness, always carry a flashlight. I keep mine in the basket in the stern along with a pair of binoculars. If you are wondering what sighting glasses have to do with fishing it is simply this: There may be times when fishing is slow, when scanning the water surface will provide clues to where fish are. I can think of dozens of occasions when I have spotted baitfish in a flight of panic on the surface. Binoculars have often saved the day and brought some fine bass to net. And don't forget the art of bird-dogging, that is, watching other fishermen who may be catching fish. It is not unsporting; it is wise. When fishing, it is important to know everything that is going on about you. Binoculars will enable you to do this. Fortunately there are small pocketsize glasses on the market that weigh less than one pound and can be easily stored in a vest or tackle box.

Another handy device is a thermometer. You can invest in a fancy electronic device or you can spend $6.99 for a plain old-fashioned one. The choice is yours. I have used both and the cheaper device, while slower, is still very effective. It is enclosed in a tube and the tube serves to also act as a depth gauge. Simply lower it into the water and let it set for five minutes. You will not only learn the temperature of the water where you are fishing, but you will also learn the depth. The small hole in the tube encasing the thermometer allows water to enter under pressure, and the depth is measured on a small scale inscribed on the thermometer case. Fifty feet of thirty-six-pound test monofilament squidding line and an old bait-casting reel or fishing line spool to store it completes a thermometer rig.

Other handy items in a boat are a coffee can for bailing if necessary, or for simply bringing some water aboard to wash off tackle; a small nylon bag with spare spark plugs; and an adjustable wrench and screwdriver for any emergency motor repairs. Lucky for us, many small outboard motors now come complete with a small tool kit that is kept under the cowling.

RODS, REELS, LINE

I have a few tricks that I employ with my tackle. Perhaps it is a bit compulsive, but I mark most of my fishing rods to assure that I can quickly measure the length of a fish. If it does not meet the minimum size limit, back it goes pronto. To do this, simply measure off from the grip check of the rod ten inches and mark it with a piece of rod winding tape. From that point, mark increments of one inch up to sixteen inches. This will normally be sufficient to measure the legal length of most fish in our area. Not only will this keep you safely within the law, but also it will allow you to quickly release a short fish without injury to it.

Fishing from a Kayak has become very popular.

As mentioned in earlier sections of this book, I have built a long rod for trout fishing. This rod, which I call the Jonah rod, is comprised of an eight-foot fly rod blank rated for a number seven fly line. The line rating is important because it suggests that there is enough backbone in the rod to set a hook. To this fly rod blank I built an ultra-light spinning reel handle with a fixed reel seat. Agate guides complete the rod. Eight guides plus a tip top guide are used, with two being affixed to the butt section and the rest set at eight inches apart over the length of the tip section.

This rod is ideal for trout in a stream or lake, and shad, and panfish. It is exceptional for casting a bubble and fly combination. With this rod, which differs from stiffer steelhead rods, four-pound test line can be used safely with the largest of fish. The drag can be set lightly, since the rod will absorb the surges of a battling fish. It is a much more pleasurable rod to use than a short, ultra-light rod. For those who choose not to build their own rod, a seven-foot, medium action rod is best for all types of trout fishing. I must confess though that I usually bring along rods as short as six feet as well, especially if I intend to cast lures for trout.

Reels are an entity unto themselves. In an earlier chapter I discussed my favorite reel. Although not much can be done to reels, there are a few tips to keep in mind. Keep them clean and well oiled. Always carry a small can of a waterproofing and lubricating agent, such as WD-40, to lubricate and clean the reel. This medium offers some protection from the elements, especially water. Mark the spool to enable yourself to know what pound test line you are using. Carry a spare spool filled with a heavier or lighter line than that being used. Always fish with the anti-reverse mechanism on. It will not hurt the reel. Most important, get to know your drag system. Be able to tell just how much pressure is exerted on the spool when you turn the drag knob.

As far as line is concerned, I prefer Berkley Trilene monofilament lines. I use clear blue and the high visibility blue line when bass fishing. I also like the green ultra low visibility Trilene XL line that I use primarily for trout fishing. Line weights I prefer are eight to ten pound test for bass and four to six pound test for trout. I buy bulk spools, which cuts down the expense compared to buying small spool fillers and I change my line frequently. To change line frequently does not mean that you have to strip the entire spool. I simply remove one hundred yards of line and splice on a fresh one hundred yards by using an Albright knot. This excellent knot is used to secure two monofilament lines together. The knot is simple to tie. Just follow the drawing on page 123.

Keep monofilament line in a dark, dry place for storage. If you keep your rod in a trunk, or (I cannot imagine this) on the deck near the rear window, you are looking for line troubles. Monofilament line dries out, cracks, and deteriorates in sunlight.

Try to think of the last time that you ever caught a fish in fresh water that required one hundred yards of line. Chances are that you have never had the need for more than fifty yards of line. The rest simply fills the spool and is on hand for an emergency, the type of which we have all imagined. There is no need to strip line from the entire spool each time you replace line.

Fold heavier test line
Loop lighter test line 8 turns
Pass end through loop
Moisten, draw tight
(Same weight lines, fold line to reel,
loop new line)

YES: End drawn to side

NO: End drawn to bottom of knot

ALBRIGHT KNOT FOR JOINING MONOFILAMENT LINE

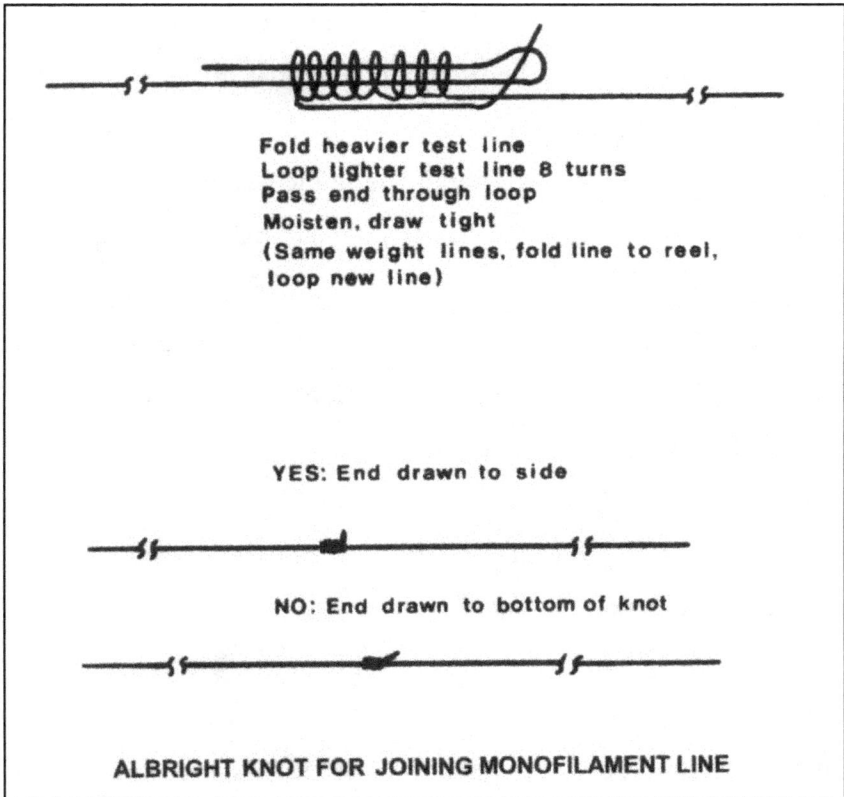

MISCELLANEOUS ITEMS

Tackle boxes are simply a place to store lures, hooks, and sundry items that we feel we need to catch fish. Usually they are well designed and come in such a large variety of styles that we need not make any great changes. The only thing that I do to my tackle box is to mark it so I can measure a fish quickly. However, many tackle boxes now come with a ruler molded into the cover. So as far as tackle boxes are concerned, I simply make sure that my name and address are printed on the inside cover. On the outside cover, I place a strip of reflective tape. When unloading a boat at night it is all too easy to forget a tackle box that was left on the shore while other chores were being done. Scanning the launch area with a flashlight before leaving will cause the reflective tape to make the box stand out sharply.

There are many uses for reflective tape. I place a small strip near the tiptop guide of my bait fishing spinning rods so that I can keep a sharp eye on them at dusk. For this purpose, white is the best color. I place red reflective tape on the stern and bow of my boat. I use reflective tape for my boat nets, boat loaders, and motors. It is an inexpensive little item that can save the day or even your life under extreme circumstances.

Pins and needles may seem to be more appropriate for a seamstress than a fisherman. Yet I use them regularly for fishing. I always carry a large needle to aid me in tying that old favorite, the nail knot. The nail knot is much more easily tied using a large needle than a nail. I carry a small needle to poke the head cement from the eye of a fly that I might have failed to clear at the tying bench. I use safety pins to hold swivels of all sorts and to keep such items together so that they don't scatter all over the well of my tackle box. They are handy on a fishing vest, shirt, or any other clothing.

I always carry a small note pad and a felt marker pen for taking notes or drawing a hotspot of a pond that I have discovered to be exceptional. You ought not to trust your discoveries to the vagaries of memory.

When trolling for trout, I have found over the years that compartmentalized plastic parts boxes are ideal. They hold a great many flies, are of clear plastic so that fly selection is easy, and they are inexpensive. Now days new and very useful tackle bags with pockets are available. They hold anywhere from four to eight plastic boxes of various sizes. When trolling with flies, I carry at least two large boxes and two small ones. The large boxes contain streamers and the smaller ones hold wet flies. This makes selection even simpler. There is no need to search through several boxes for a fly.

Other useful storage items, especially for trout fishing, are small, round stack-pack containers. These safely store hooks, swivels, and split shots. Best of all, they can be stored in a jacket or vest pocket when necessary.

SPECIAL EQUIPMENT

Over the years I have found some handy gadgets that have helped me while fishing. Fisherman's tackle bags are available, for example that come with a shoulder strap for easy carrying. As stated earlier they can be purchased in any number of combinations of pockets and sizes to accommodate fishermen's needs. I prefer the nylon bags with zippered side pockets and room for at least four plastic tackle boxes inside the main compartment. My choice of size is fourteen inches wide by ten inches deep by eight and one-half inches high.

In my bag I keep two fly reels, two medium size fly boxes, spare leader material, plastic bubbles, bobbers, a can of dry fly spray, a can of fly line dressing, two plastic stack packs with hooks and sinkers, a large needle for tying nail knots, two safety pins holding assorted swivels, a spinning reel, a flashlight, a thermometer, spinning lure box. In the side pockets, I keep two fly reel spools, a spare spinning reel spool, stringers, a spare spool of fishing line, a lead-core line reel, a small can of spray on repellant, a small first aid kit, and a small sewing kit.

In my bass bag, I keep four plastic boxes complete with all the lures I will need on any outing. In the side pouches is a pair of pliers, a combination scale to measure and weight fish, a small first aid kit, stringer, knife, insect repellent and a flashlight.

Another handy bag is a canvas tote bag. I often carry a large one in which I place my fisherman's bag. I also store in it a fishing vest, rain gear, lunch, camera and a variety of other small items. These bags retail for about twenty dollars and will last for years with little care. They are strong and waterproof. When it starts to rain, I often use the bag to protect my cameras by folding the sides over.

A fisherman's pliers with a side cutter are one of the most important pieces of equipment an angler can own. It has a side cutter that can cut both monofilament and wire. It can also be used to cut hooks, and the pliers' flat jaw has a small slot to hold split shot while being compressed. With a case, the pliers cost less than twelve dollars and are a worthy investment.

French snaps are ideal for attaching landing nets to a vest. I secure one to my landing net used for wading. The French snap is a device that opens when you squeeze it in the middle. This is useful when you are reaching for a landing net that is hanging on your back. I also apply a French snap to my wading staff so that I may easily secure it to my vest when not actually moving about. These are available at most hardware stores.

Polarized sunglasses are a must while fishing. These glasses will enable you to see what the shoreline structure looks like, and to spot a fish long before it approaches the net. They will also aid you in locating rocks and boulders when fishing in larger glacial lakes. Those pristine bodies of water that harbor lunker smallmouth bass are usually rock strewn and dangerous.

A good hat is a must. Most of today's adjustable hats are fine. They are well ventilated for hot weather fishing. However, those with long visors are best. They shade the eyes and aid in peering into the water when using polarized sunglasses. These inexpensive caps will also prevent serious sunstroke problems on a hot day. In colder weather, the same type of hat without ventilating holes is best.

Insect repellents should always be on hand during the late spring and through the summer. I carry both spray-on and rub-on repellents with me whenever I go astream. The spray-on is usually kept in the tackle box or fishing bag and the rub-on carried in a vest pocket.

There is nothing worse than having a good evening of fishing spoiled because of mosquitoes or gnats. There are too many fine repellents on the market at reasonable prices to be without some form of protection.

There are a number of tools that we pick up over the years to enhance our fishing. These are a few of mine and they have served me well.

SHORE FISHING EQUIPMENT

Boats are not the only places fishermen fish from. They are most practical, but there have been many times when I chose to fish for trout from the shore. Fortunately, there is not too much equipment needed for shore fishing. Most of the tackle we employ while boat fishing is suitable for shore fishing. There are some devices that can make shore fishing a bit easier and more enjoyable and it would be wise to discuss these few small items.

Rod spikes or holders are a must when fishing from the shore. They keep our rods set at a good angle to the water. They keep the reel out of the sand and the rod out from underfoot. Most important, they are far more efficient than using a cut sapling. The time you waste searching for and cutting a sapling can better be used for fishing.

I have tried several types of rod holders for shore fishing. The best I have found are simple two-piece devices. They can be taken apart when not in use and slipped together easily when needed. They are made of galvanized steel, are sturdy, and have a sharp spike made of angled steel to insert into the toughest of terrain. Most important, they keep the reels fairly high off the ground so that they can be placed near the water.

A fine shore fishing tool is the Cape Cod rod holder, described in detail on page 170. It is a tall rod holder capable of being placed out into the water to enable fishermen to cast further offshore and still keep their rods high and dry and highly visible.

Another handy piece of equipment for shore fishing is a seat. I use two types at various times. One is a nylon seat with a pouch. It collapses and has a strap to facilitate carrying. In this seat I can carry baits, tackle, camera, and a host of items I may find useful once I arrive at my fishing destination. I sometimes use a bucket seat made of hard plastic that has two trays for tackle and a small cooler for bait or refreshment.

Seats are not for lazy fishermen. They are for practical anglers. They not only allow you to rest while shore fishing, but can be used to carry tackle astream. This is especially important when the hotspot is some distance from your car or truck.

Another gadget that I have used for shore fishing is a rope stringer with a metal tip to insert into the ground. I use a large size stringer approximately twenty-four inches long because the metal tip is longer and sticks further into the ground. Such stringers will safely hold large fish or full limits of fish. These I use when fishing during the springtime when the water is cool enough to keep the fish without any spoilage.

Because wading has been discussed in previous sections I won't discuss wading again. But I will mention that whenever you are shore fishing it is a good idea to wear hip boots or at least rubberized calf-length boots. It is better to wade out to land a hefty trout than to drag it ashore. Fish can get leverage when they are dragged into shallow water and a hook that is not securely imbedded can easily pull free. If you insist on beaching a trout, do it as follows: When you have the fish close to shore, but not in water so shallow that it is touching bottom, pull it toward shore with one quick, smooth movement. This will assure that it will be safely beached. This method is good even while boat fishing. If you have forgotten the landing net, grab the line about two feet from the fish and lift straight up and over the gunnel in one fell swoop.

7

Odds & Ends

Fly Line Splice

Deep trolling with flies is a great way to find trout any time of the year. However, in many Fly-Fishing-Only lakes and ponds, the use of lead core line, the most popular medium for deep trolling is illegal.

There is now a line available that is legal that is called Salmon Trolling Line that is a heavy, level line designed especially for trolling deep. However, there is another way to get down to the fish and stay within the law. It is to splice two fly lines together.

The accompanying drawing shows exactly how to do it. To get down deep, buy the two fastest sinking heavy weight fly lines you can and splice them together. These lines will assure that you can get down quickly.

To make the splice all you need is a small single edge razor or Exacto knife, some Super Glue, a tube of Pliobond, some fly tying thread and a bottle of red head cement.

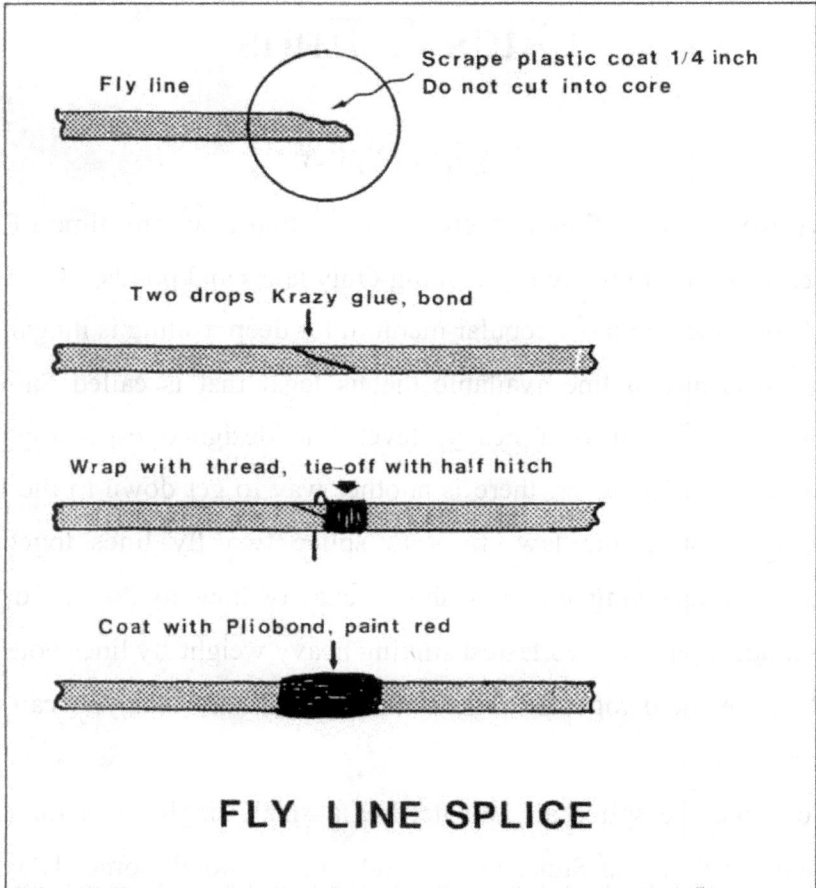

Fly line

Scrape plastic coat 1/4 inch
Do not cut into core

Two drops Krazy glue, bond

Wrap with thread, tie-off with half hitch

Coat with Pliobond, paint red

FLY LINE SPLICE

Three Top Flies

Three excellent flies in this book have local, New England origins and are not well known outside the region. I fish with these flies almost exclusively and I am presenting them here in an easy to copy form.

The Golden Demon was originally a western fly, but through the years the fly has been varied so much that now what we know as the Golden Demon here in New England is our own unique version.

Over the past 15 years I have varied the Golden Demon in an attempt to improve upon it. I am pleased to say that the small contributions to the fly have improved it greatly. Mostly these variations have to do with the wing topping. And I would like to emphasize that I do not use substitute materials when tying. I use golden pheasant crest for a tail and bronzed mallard for a wing, there is no true need to substitute these items because the few cents saved using substitute materials of lesser quality may change the fly enough to result in fewer fish.

The Demon wing should be tied sparse. When I tie them I use a small piece of the mallard feather about three-eighths of an inch wide and I fold it and tie it in. Over this wing I tie three strands of Pearlescent Flashabou, this small detail has actually doubled my catch over a plain wing. Another favorite variation introduced to me by my fishing friend Paul Sawyer is to tie three to four strands of gold Krystal Flash over the wing. For the five years that I have used this gold wing topping it has proven to be excellent.

Here is a tip: Tie all your demons with these wing toppings. If you choose to use a Demon with the plain mallard wing you can simply snip off these flashy materials. However, if your fly box has plain winged Demons only, and you feel a need for some flash, you could be out of luck.

Tie the Demon flies no larger than size eight or smaller than size ten for trout. Always use a straight shank hook such as a Daiichi 1750 or a Mustad 9674. Straight shank hooks ride better and have excellent hooking power. The Dan's Leech is an easy to tie but very effective fly. The black leech is best; however, a green leech will work at times. This fly works best on straight shank hooks; the Mustad 9575 hook will do. The only difference between this hook and the M 36620 is that this hook has a turned down eye.

Use four strands of marabou for the body and keep the tail approximately one-half inch long. A secret with this fly is that the shabbier it becomes from fish striking it the better it works. This fly can also be tied with wire to weight it down.

The T-Bone is a great fly and employs some great fish attracting materials. The brown hackle used as a rib should be trimmed close on top of the body but left a bit longer in the belly section. A small section of lemon wood flank feather about three-eighths of an inch wide should be folded and tied in as the wing. This fly is best is sizes ten and twelve, but do tie some in a size eight as well, especially if you choose to troll with it.

Three Top Flies

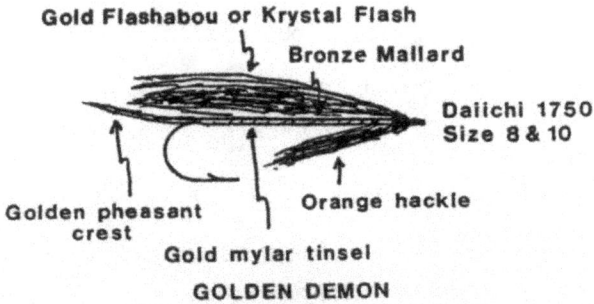

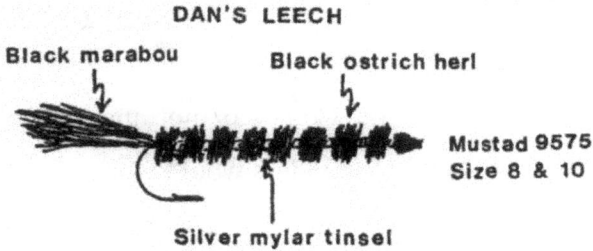

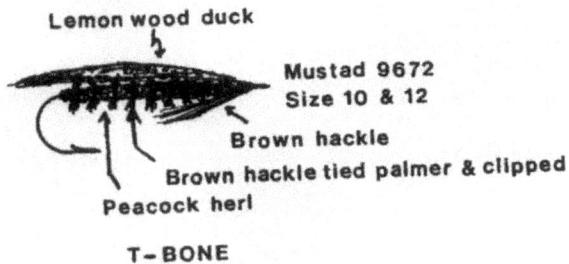

Gold Flashabou or Krystal Flash

Bronze Mallard

Daiichi 1750
Size 8 & 10

Golden pheasant
crest

Orange hackle

Gold mylar tinsel

GOLDEN DEMON

DAN'S LEECH

Black marabou

Black ostrich herl

Mustad 9575
Size 8 & 10

Silver mylar tinsel

Lemon wood duck

Mustad 9672
Size 10 & 12

Brown hackle

Brown hackle tied palmer & clipped

Peacock herl

T–BONE

Cape Cod Rod Holder

About 15 years ago, I saw several men including a fishing friend of mine using tall rod holders that they stuck into the sand several feet from shore. These were the very same type rod holders that I had seen two decades previous while fishing Cape Cod ponds.

The rod holders were designed to stick in the sandy shelf that is a trademark of Cape Cod's kettle ponds. These ponds were created by retreating glaciers at the end of the last ice age. Did you know that; occurring at intervals of once every 10,000 years or so, we're overdue for another ice agew? Some scientists have even speculated that due to the effects of global warming, we have actually stopped the onset of the next ice age.

It was obvious that Cape Cod was not the only geographical location where these great rod holders would work.

These special rod holders are four feet tall. This is to allow a fisherman to wade out to the edge of a shallow shoreline and cast into a deep drop off. The rod can then be placed in the tall rod holder while the fisherman can relax.

I have used this Cape Cod rod holder in all sorts of varied locations. Whenever I plan to fish from shore, a pair of these rod holders is taken with me in case I need them.

The rod holder is simple to make but it doesn't hurt if you have a friend who can do a bit of welding for you. The materials are relatively inexpensive and easy to come by. A Cape Cod rod holder will cost roughly four to five dollars to make and maybe less if you already have the pipe.

The pipe material can be either copper or steel piping three-quarter inches in diameter and four feet long. The only other materials needed are two one-quarter inch steel rods.

At the top of the rod holder one piece of steel rod is bent in a curved shape to accept a spinning rod handle. At the bottom end the other steel rod acts as the spike to stick into the ground. This 12- inch piece of steel rod should be sharpened to penetrate the bottom easily. Four inches should be inserted and epoxied into the pipe and eight inches should be left to penetrate the bottom.

Two inches from the pipe a five-inch piece of steel rod should be welded across the spike to prevent the rod holder from twisting. Both the spike and the spinning handle holder are attached to the pipe with epoxy.

The pipe can be painted and usually is by many fishermen. Painting is optional and may or may not prevent the pipes from eroding.

Pipe length can be slightly longer sometimes up to five feet, but longer than that is not suggested. It takes little time and money to make one of these most useful and practical rod holders. I can safely predict that more than a few of the waters where you do your fishing are likely to be ideally suited for using the Cape Code rod holder.

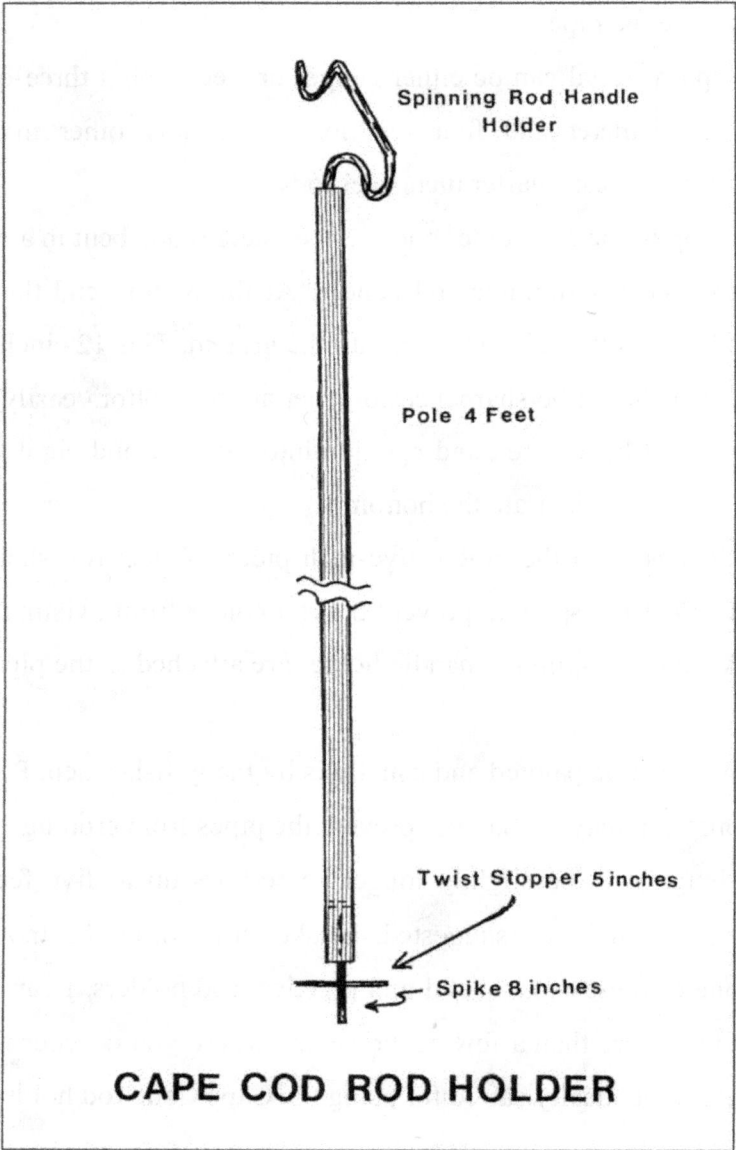

Spinning Rod Handle
Holder

Pole 4 Feet

Twist Stopper 5 inches

Spike 8 inches

CAPE COD ROD HOLDER

Ice Fishing Trap

Ice fishing is more popular than ever for many reasons. Perhaps it is because new modern cold weather gear at affordable prices makes it easier for people to enter the sport. Or perhaps it is because ice fishing can be a very social form of fishing. One wherein many people can fish a crowded lake and not be disturbed by the nearness of other fishermen.

No matter what your reason for joining the ice fishing fraternity there are a few things that you can do to make your ice fishing a bit more interesting and successful. One is to set your ice fishing traps up properly. For this reason, how to make your ice fishing traps more effective and different from most other fishermen is herein presented.

Most ice fishing devices cost less than ten dollars. Even those with spools that are fully wound with line can be purchased for less than fifteen dollars. No matter whether you prefer to spool you own line or not, one thing is important. Use nylon squidding line or buy traps with nylon squidding line already wound to the spool. Because it is impervious to rot, nylon squidding line will last a lifetime of ice fishing. Stay clear of that ugly green and gray twine line.

I paint my ice fishing traps fluorescent orange. To do this simply requires painting the upright shaft of the cross bar type traps white, then applying two coats of fluorescent orange paint. Doing this makes the traps highly visible under most lighting conditions. And since most fishermen do not paint their traps, your traps will be easily identified when you are fishing a tournament or in a crowd.

I also remove the small flags that usually come with the traps and place a larger orange flag in its place. I number each of the flags of my traps from one through six. The reason for numbering the flags is so that I can know what size bait I have on each flag.

I usually buy mixed bait with half-large shiners and half medium. This assures that even if there are only small fish around I will have some action. The numbering of the flags serves me thus; if I am using medium shiners on flags one through three and large shiners on four and five, I know when a flag is tripped which ones have the larger bait. Therefore, I watch more carefully before attempting to set the hook on the larger baited traps. It is not foolproof because small perch are daring enough to consume a large shiner but this numbering of the flags has helped me to catch some big bass and pickerel through the years.

To the tag end of the squidding line apply a small shirt button. This will act as a depth marker when you set your bait. I paint my buttons fluorescent red so that I can see them easily, however it is not necessary to do so. It is important to have a button as a depth marker, however.

After the button has been slipped onto the line a size ten-barrel swivel should be tied to the tag end of the squidding line. To the free end of the swivel tie on three feet of ten or fourteen pound test monofilament. The line strength you choose to use should be determined by the species that you are fishing for and your optimism for catching big fish.

A short shank size one or two hook should be tied on next. If pickerel are your target you might be better off with a long shank hook but these have never been my favorites. One foot above the hook apply a 3/0 split shot. Your trap is now ready for action.

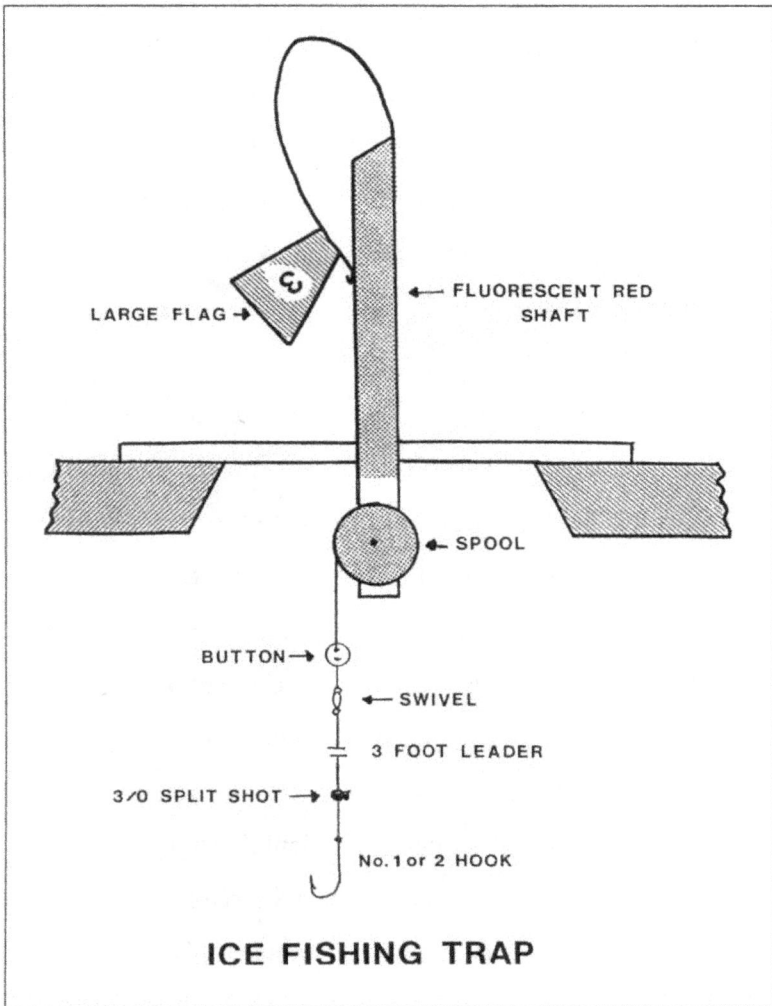

LARGE FLAG →

← FLUORESCENT RED SHAFT

← SPOOL

BUTTON →

← SWIVEL

3 FOOT LEADER

3/0 SPLIT SHOT →

No. 1 or 2 HOOK

ICE FISHING TRAP

Shad Darts

The popularity of fishing for shad seems to be increasing each year, at least in my region.

Rigging terminal tackle for shad is easy. Because this fish is almost unpredictable at times seeming to strike any lure in front of it one day and nothing the next, it is important to be ready with several terminal rigs. To begin, shad are mostly caught with shad darts. This is a lead head jig with a hair or nylon skirt. Most knowledgeable fishermen know that the skirt is not necessary at all. It is necessary only because it attracts buyers. If you plan to paint your own or mold your own do not be concerned about a skirt.

The most important thing to note about a shad dart is that it must have a gold hook to be effective. And for most shad fishing a small dart is better than a larger one. Nowadays some fishermen, this author included, employ what is known as a magnum dart, which is just slightly larger than the one-quarter ounce size dart.

My favorites darts are 1/32 and 1/16-ounce sizes. Once herring come into the river and begin to strike the smaller dart I use larger size darts. I also go to larger one-eighth and one-quarter ounce sizes when the water is high. When striped bass are around, I use a magnum size in hope of catching an incidental striper.

You can use two darts in tandem to increase your chances of hooking up. For those who choose to quickly release their shad, a dangling hook can present a hazard. When using two darts it is best to attach a ¼-ounce dart to a snap swivel and a 1/8 or 1/16-ounce dart to the first dart via 18 - 24 inches of monofilament.

Another tandem method is to attach a simple gold hook 18-inches from the dart whether it is a ¼ or 1/8-ounce dart. Other trailers that are used successfully are small bright red or orange pieces of chenille tied to a gold hook.

My favorite rig is a one-quarter ounce egg sinker above a small barrel swivel. On the terminal end of the swivel I attach 24-inches of six-pound monofilament line to which I attach a 1/32 or 1/8-ounce red dart sans skirt. Shad usually strike in spurts, but where you are fishing is very important. Often one fisherman may have all the action while another goes without a strike. Later, the table will turn as the shad move on. Different locations will also play into the scheme as shad often follow set patterns when traveling upstream.

My favorite color for shad is bright red. Chartreuse, white, and yellow follow this. I have used unpainted shad darts and caught them. Color may vary day to day but the most consistent color and size is the bright red 1/32 dart.

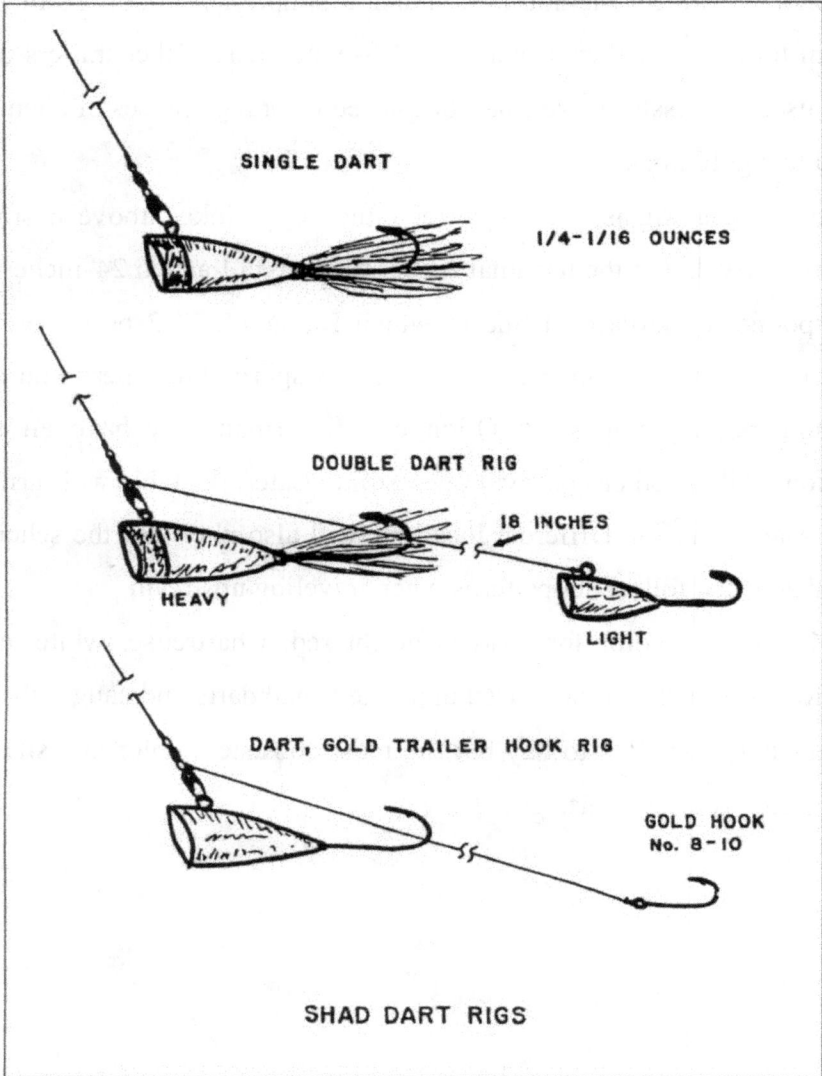

SINGLE DART

1/4-1/16 OUNCES

DOUBLE DART RIG

18 INCHES

HEAVY

LIGHT

DART, GOLD TRAILER HOOK RIG

GOLD HOOK
No. 8-10

SHAD DART RIGS

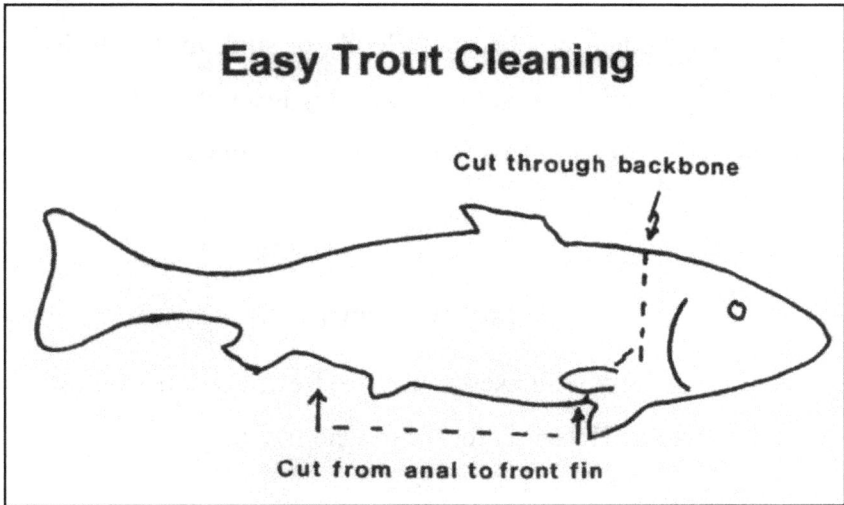

Insert finger into backbone and pull head down. Head, entrails and pectoral fin are removed in one piece. To remove blood line inside, scrape with knife.

Keeping & Cooking Fish

In spring it is usually safe to keep trout on a stringer for short periods of time. As the weather warms and the water surface temperature increases, usually by mid-May, it is best to ice trout immediately. Icing the fish in a cooler will prevent spoilage and keep the flesh fresh and firm

Because trout are small scaled fish they are prone to spoil more easily than fish such as carp or bass. This is one reason why all small-scaled fish should be handled carefully if they are to be eaten.

You can tell if fish are fresh by watching for certain signs. If the fish is in a stage of rigor mortis for example it is fresh. If the gills are bright red it is fresh. Gills will pale as time wears on and become very pink. The eyes should be clear not cloudy or sunk in. Fresh fish will smell fresh, if they have a strong odor they are not fresh. And fresh fish should feel firm when poked not soft to the touch.

Tinfoil Trout

This recipe is one my wife uses to prepare fresh trout. It's quick, easy, and delicious. Here it is for those who like to grill their food.

Lay two trout on aluminum foil.

Baste each fish inside and out with butter.

Chop onions peppers and tomatoes.

Place the ingredients in the tinfoil on top of the trout.

Add garlic powder and sprinkle soy sauce on all the ingredients.

Close the aluminum foil around the fish by folding it into a pouch.

Grill on medium heat for 20 to 25 minutes.

Setting Up Your Fishing Log

A fishing log will serve to increase a fisherman's catch from year to year. I have used a log for over three decades and it has paid off handsomely. The few minutes each evening that it takes to jot down that day's fishing events will improve your future fishing and actually allow you more fishing time in the future.

Through the years I have relied on my logs to aid me in deciding when to take a fishing trip, when to start fishing a certain pond or river and what weather conditions offered me the best fishing. My logs have been invaluable to me and to this day I still keep records of my fishing.

Here is how I set up my fishing log. You may want to add or delete some items but once you have designed a page you can simply have copies made. A loose-leaf binder is ideal for storing these valuable pages of information.

Fishing Log

Date_____

Time_____

Weather_____

Partner(s)_____

Where_____

Shore/Boat_____

No. of Fish caught_____

Species_____

Best lure/Bait_____

Notes _____

_____

_____

_____

I keep my log simple; the notes section usually covers most of what I might need to know for future use over and above the log entries.

Useful Gadgets for Fishermen

Steel shower curtain rings are very useful to store items that I often use when fishing. They attach easily to the D rings of today's new tackle bags. Items such as nail clippers, forceps, a GI can opener, or a small ruler or scale are just a few of the uses you can find for this small item.

Small plastic snap lid food containers are a handy item to store corn, mealworms, and marshmallows. These will keep the baits fresh and can be placed in a refrigerator without cause to worry because of their tight lids. In cold temperatures, mealworms lay dormant.

Women's arts and crafts stores are great places for fly fishermen to browse. Many of the items found in these stores are useful for fishermen. The paints sold for shirt designs can be used for the heads of fishing flies. The color selection offers great choices for innovation. The specialty glitter that is available in many colors is great for enhancing Power Bait and lures. And some of the small tools such as tweezers, snippers and scissors are ideal for fly tying.

A picture is truly worth a thousand words. For this reason a small pocket sized camera should always be part of a tackle bag. This is especially true for those who choose to catch and release. With throwaway cameras so inexpensive nowadays there is no need to bring along expensive SLR's.

Binoculars are important fishing tools. Today small pocket sized ones are available and so are monoculars. Uses for these are to watch for rising fish; scouting bird activity, which often denotes a hatch of flies, and to see what fellow fishermen, are doing.

Inexpensive two-way radios are a great help if you and a fishing partner are fishing a stream or in separate boats. They are also useful when you are at a lake on vacation to let the family know where on a lake you are or if you will be returning to the dock.

I sometimes use rangefinder, the type archers use to measure distance to the target. I use mine to take my bearings on a lake or pond where relocating a spring hole is critical. These tools are expensive but often worthwhile owning.

Kayaks

Fishing from a kayak is becoming very popular. While I have never been one who enjoyed fishing from canoes, I now have a kayak. The reason I decided to try one of these ancient crafts is because they offer fishermen who often fish alone a chance to carry a boat into some small remote ponds and streams.

My kayak for example is not one of those especially designed for fishing. My choice of kayak was primarily based on size and weight. It is but ten feet long and weighs only thirty-five pounds. There are longer, heavier kayaks on the market such as the Walden Scout that is better suited for fishing due to its stability and the fact that it has a cooler for refreshment or tackle.

To make my kayak (a Walden Experience model) more suitable for fishing I have affixed two short bungee cord tie downs to each side of the cockpit. These are used to secure the paddle while I am fishing and the rod while I am paddling. Having a bungee cord on each side is extremely convenient and for the price of five dollars per set they are a good investment.

The kayak has a compartment in the rear to hold equipment and bungee cords in front to store extra equipment that would not fit into the rear compartment. I use this front bungee cord set up to hold my landing net.

To make the kayak more useable I have installed a small anchor and pulley system so that I might lower and raise the anchor from the cockpit. The small grapple type anchor weighs a pound and is for small ponds. A heavier three-pound anchor is available for river fishing. The anchor system with anchor, rope, and hardware sells for approximately $30.

I have installed a rod holder so that I can fish while paddling. The best rod holder is one with a flush mount. This mount is capped so that no water can enter when a rod holder is not installed. I have both a spinning rod holder and one for a fly rod. Rod holders and mounts range anywhere from $20 to $30.

I never use the work deck, which is a nylon skirt for the cockpit. Instead I use a good life preserver complete with pockets in which I carry those flies or lures I will need for an outing.

Lures For Trolling For Trout

Trolling for trout doesn't always mean dragging a fly behind a boat. Indeed, on many occasions when trout fail to strike a fly, a lure will save the day. One of the very best lures for trolling for trout is a Super Duper.

For trout, sizes 501, 502, and 503 are best. At times larger ones will work, but most often these sizes in gold or silver will bring trout to the net. Fluorescent red and copper colored ones should also be a part of the Super Duper selection.

While many fishermen do not impart any movement to a Super Duper while trolling, sweeping the rod back and forth adds a bit more action to the lure. Very often it is during the downward fall of the lure that trout strike.

When playing a fish with the Super Duper be aware that you must maintain a tight line. It is not uncommon to lose a fish once even a slight bit of slack is present. Very often when a trout is netted, the Super Duper falls out of the trout's jaw. This is because of the slack that develops when the trout is scooped up.

Other fine lures for trolling for trout are the Mooselook Wobbler in the smaller sizes, the Al's Goldfish, the Colorado in brass and gold and copper and gold, and Little Cleo spoon in gold. One-sixth to one quarter ounce sizes are best.

The use of a high quality swivel is best for trolling lures to prevent line twist whether using a fly rod and lead cored line or a spinning rod with monofilament line.

While determining depth with lead cored line is easy due to the color-coding of the line, which changes every ten yards, it is more difficult to do with a monofilament line. There are line counters to allow fishermen to know how much line is played out but there is a simpler method that does not require a counter. Simply cast the lure out as far as you can and hen as the line tightens sweep the rod back several times counting the sweeps. This way once the fish are located you're back at the same depth.

Shore Fishing

Fishing for trout from shore is mostly a springtime event. Once the water warms trout move into deeper areas of a lake or pond. Much further than an angler using an heavy egg sinker rig can cast.

However, during the early part of the trout season from ice out in northern climes and early March in other areas of the country, trout do frequent shorelines. It is during this period shore fishermen do catch plenty of trout.

The bubble and fly technique described earlier is one way to make the best of shoreline fishing in spring. However, many fishermen opt to use bait and wait patiently for a bite.

To assure that bait can be cast a long distance to trout cruising the shoreline the following bottom fishing rig is ideal. Slip on a one-quarter or half ounce egg sinker to the tag end of the fishing line. Add a small size ten-barrel swivel so that the egg sinker can slide no further than the swivel. To the free end of the barrel swivel, tie on 18 inches of leader. The best hook size for power bait is a size eight egg hook. These hooks hold Power Bait well. There is no need to use a treble hook when using power bait.

Once the bait is cast out and settles to the bottom take in some slack but not all. Draw down the line and place a bobber on it. Some commercial fluorescent colored bobbers are now made that have weight to allow them to be cast. However, I add a large split shot via of a short piece of monofilament to one end of the bobber for more weight. To the end of the bobber to be attached to the fishing line I clip on a half of a paper clip, leaving the clip to the line open enough so that it easily comes off the line. When a fish takes the bait the bobber will be drawn up signaling the take.

Chumming with corn, which is legal in many states, is a good way to attract fish. Shore fishermen who do not have the throwing arm of a big league baseball pitcher might just as well forget it. However, there is a way to chum from shore that works. I have used a slingshot to get my chum offshore for many years. The slingshot has a pliable basket capable of holding a small handful of corn kernels. Depending on how far back the slingshot is drawn the corn can be hurled a great distance. The slingshot is relatively inexpensive at $12 and well worth the investment.

Any number of rod holders on the market will do a good job of minding the rod while the fisherman relaxes on his seat. A simple and inexpensive one I use is of spiral metal and holds the lower part of the rod handle. It allows for a quick pick up of the rod. At times I also employ a large rod holder than can accommodate three rods. Using two such rod holders when carp fishing from shore allows me to keep the rods parallel to the ground while using bait runner reels.

One essential tool for shore fishermen is a comfortable chair or stool. I prefer the type that have two compartments one on each side to store equipment. By being able to carry all the necessary tackle in the compartments I can easily tote my tackle long distances.

Rod-holders free up your hands and allow you to run more than one rod

This portable seat doubles as a tackle box!

Roger Aziz

Outdoors writer for *Eagle-Tribune newspapers* and *Methuen Life*

Published in:

> *The New England Fisherman*
> *Bass Angler's Sportsman's Society magazine*
> *Flyfisher magazine*
> *New England Outdoors*

Member:

> New England Outdoor Writers Association (former director)
> B.A.S.S.
> National Rifle Association

Fishing for over 50 years in New England waters, both fresh and salt.

Married, with three sons: Wife Shirley, sons Roger Jr., David and Steven

AnEx Publications

www.anexpub.com

www.ingramcontent.com/pod-product-compliance
Lightning Source LLC
Chambersburg PA
CBHW070806100426
42742CB00012B/2272